# Angola

# WORLD BIBLIOGRAPHICAL SERIES
General Editors:
Robert G. Neville (Executive Editor)
John J. Horton

Robert A. Myers                    Ian Wallace
Hans H. Wellisch          Ralph Lee Woodward, Jr.

**John J. Horton** is Deputy Librarian of the University of Bradford and currently Chairman of its Academic Board of Studies in Social Sciences. He has maintained a longstanding interest in the discipline of area studies and its associated bibliographical problems, with special reference to European Studies. In particular he has published in the field of Icelandic and of Yugoslav studies, including the two relevant volumes in the World Bibliographical Series.

**Robert A. Myers** is Associate Professor of Anthropology in the Division of Social Sciences and Director of Study Abroad Programs at Alfred University, Alfred, New York. He has studied post-colonial island nations of the Caribbean and has spent two years in Nigeria on a Fulbright Lectureship. His interests include international public health, historical anthropology and developing societies. In addition to *Amerindians of the Lesser Antilles: a bibliography* (1981), *A Resource Guide to Dominica, 1493-1986* (1987) and numerous articles, he has compiled the World Bibliographical Series volumes on *Dominica* (1987), *Nigeria* (1989) and *Ghana* (1991).

**Ian Wallace** is Professor of German at the University of Bath. A graduate of Oxford in French and German, he also studied in Tübingen, Heidelberg and Lausanne before taking teaching posts at universities in the USA, Scotland and England. He specializes in contemporary German affairs, especially literature and culture, on which he has published numerous articles and books. In 1979 he founded the journal *GDR Monitor*, which he continues to edit under its new title *German Monitor*.

**Hans H. Wellisch** is Professor emeritus at the College of Library and Information Services, University of Maryland. He was President of the American Society of Indexers and was a member of the International Federation for Documentation. He is the author of numerous articles and several books on indexing and abstracting, and has published *The Conversion of Scripts* and *Indexing and Abstracting: an International Bibliography*. He also contributes frequently to *Journal of the American Society for Information Science, The Indexer* and other professional journals.

**Ralph Lee Woodward, Jr.** is Director of Graduate Studies at Tulane University, New Orleans, where he has been Professor of History since 1970. He is the author of *Central America, a Nation Divided*, 2nd ed. (1985), as well as several monographs and more than sixty scholarly articles on modern Latin America. He has also compiled volumes in the World Bibliographical Series on *Belize* (1980), *Nicaragua* (1983) and *El Salvador* (1988). Dr. Woodward edited the Central American section of the *Research Guide to Central America and the Caribbean* (1985) and is currently editor of the Central American history section of the *Handbook of Latin American Studies*.

VOLUME 151

# Angola

### Richard Black

*Compiler*

## CLIO PRESS

OXFORD, ENGLAND · SANTA BARBARA, CALIFORNIA
DENVER, COLORADO

British Library Cataloguing in Publication Data

Angola. – (World bibliographical series; v.151)
I. Black, Richard    II. Series
016.9673


ISBN 1–85109–143–2


Clio Press Ltd.,
55 St. Thomas' Street,
Oxford OX1 1JG, England.

ABC-CLIO,
130 Cremona Drive,
Santa Barbara,
CA 93116, USA.


Designed by Bernard Crossland.
Typeset by Columns Design and Production Services Ltd, Reading, England.
Printed and bound in Great Britain by
Bookcraft (Bath) Ltd., Midsomer Norton.

# THE WORLD BIBLIOGRAPHICAL SERIES

This series, which is principally designed for the English speaker, will eventually cover every country (and many of the world's principal regions), each in a separate volume comprising annotated entries on works dealing with its history, geography, economy and politics; and with its people, their culture, customs, religion and social organization. Attention will also be paid to current living conditions – housing, education, newspapers, clothing, etc.– that are all too often ignored in standard bibliographies; and to those particular aspects relevant to individual countries. Each volume seeks to achieve, by use of careful selectivity and critical assessment of the literature, an expression of the country and an appreciation of its nature and national aspirations, to guide the reader towards an understanding of its importance. The keynote of the series is to provide, in a uniform format, an interpretation of each country that will express its culture, its place in the world, and the qualities and background that make it unique. The views expressed in individual volumes, however, are not necessarily those of the publisher.

## VOLUMES IN THE SERIES

# Contents

**Contents**

Contents

# Introduction

Over the last three decades, Angola has been embroiled in one of Africa's longest-running conflicts. Since fighting began in 1961, first against the Portuguese, and subsequently between rival liberation movements, each with its own superpower backers, research in Angola has been difficult, if not impossible. Meanwhile, since independence, the collapse of the country's infrastructure as a result of the war and external aggression, coupled with economic mismanagement, and a shortage of skilled workers, has scared away much foreign investment. An end to the conflict is clearly long overdue for the Angolan people, who have suffered greatly over the last three decades. However, should the temporary peace which preceded democratic elections in September 1992 prove more permanent, this should also provide an opportunity both for renewed overseas involvement to assist in the country's recovery, and for research, into a vastly interesting and wealthy country.

This volume aims to provide a basis from which the casual reader, businessman, or academic specialist, can begin to access the more readily available information on Angola. Given the recent history of the country, accurate statistical information is hard to come by, whilst political and historical work is often imbued with the fierce ideological struggle that has been waging since independence and before. However, beyond these difficulties, there lies a wealth of material too – not always easily accessible, and often problematic in its own way, but of great interest. It is not pretended here that a complete or comprehensive listing of this material has been possible: indeed, some major areas of work have been excluded on grounds of generality or language as discussed below. Similarly, this introduction aims to provide a basis from which to approach this material, although again without any claim to being a fully authoritative account.

## Geography and climate

Angola is the sixth largest country in Africa, spanning from tropical rain forest in the north, to the Namib desert in the south. With an estimated population of around 10.5 million people, it is also one of the least populated countries of sub-Saharan Africa, with a population density of around 8.5 per km$^2$. Of this vast land area, around 43 per cent is forest or woodland, with just 2.8 per cent under cultivation. However, potentially fertile agricultural land extends much further than that which is currently cultivated: indeed the country's immense agricultural potential was one of the factors which attracted over 300,000 Portuguese settlers during the late colonial period. Coupled with large-scale reserves of oil, diamonds, and iron ore, as well as huge potential for hydro-electric power generation on rivers such as the Cuanza and Cunene, Angola is potentially one of the richest countries in Africa in terms of its natural resources.

Geographically, Angola can be divided into a number of zones: at its core are the coastal areas surrounding the three towns of Luanda, Benguela and Namibe, and the highlands immediately to the east. This area is the most populous, with densities of over 12 persons per km$^2$. At its peak, the Benguela plateau reaches 2,600 m, the highest point of a chain of mountains cut by rivers running to the Atlantic coasts. In contrast, the country's fringes, the Congo basin in the north, the Upper Zambesi valley in the east, and the southern desert have population densities of nearer 2 persons per km$^2$. The east in particular consists of hill country, giving way to the flat expanses where both the Zambesi and Congo rivers originate. Rainfall shows a gradient from north to south, with the rainy season concentrated in the months from October to May. On the coast, temperatures are lower than usual in terms of latitude, as a result of the cool Benguela ocean current. Inland, temperatures are more extreme.

There are three main ethnic groups in Angola. The largest is the Ovimbundu, who make up slightly over one third of the total population. This group, who speak Umbundu, live mainly in the centre and south of the country, around the urban centres of Huambo and Bié. During the last few decades of political struggle, they have been associated with UNITA (*União Nacional de Independência Total de Angola*), one of three liberation movements active against the colonial régime. Next in terms of population comes the Mbundu, who make up around 20 per cent of the total, and are concentrated in the capital Luanda, in Malanje, and along the Cuanza valley in the centre to north of the country. This group speaks Kimbundu, and has been associated mainly with the MPLA (*Movimento Popular de Libertação de Angola*), which took power in Angola after independence.

The third ethnic group is the Bakongo of the north of the country, especially Uíge and Zaïre provinces. This group in practice spans the borders of Angola, Zaïre and the Congo republic, speaking variants of the Kikongo language. The Bakongo have been associated with the FNLA (*Frente Nacional de Libertação de Angola*), which led the first major insurrection against Portuguese rule in 1961, but was defeated militarily in 1975/76 by the MPLA. Other smaller ethnic groups include the Lunda and Chokwe in the east of the country; the Kwanyama of the southern border, who are closely associated with the Ovambo of Namibia, and a sizeable population of *mestiço* peoples: those who were assimilated with the white Portuguese settlers. This latter group live mainly in urban areas, and in particular, in Luanda.

Angola is still a predominantly rural country, although increasing numbers of people live in towns, not least because of the civil war which has disrupted normal life since independence. This reflects the sporadic and unpredictable nature of guerilla warfare, which has made urban centres the safest places in which to live. From under half a million at the time of independence, Luanda's population in particular has grown considerably, to an estimated 1.55 million in 1989, despite the exodus of Portuguese settlers. In 1985, the United Nations estimated that 24 per cent of the population were in urban areas, compared with just under 18 per cent ten years earlier.

The crude death rate in Angola remains high, at around 21 per thousand, with infant mortality standing at 137 per thousand live births. It is estimated that over 300,000 have died as a direct result of the war since independence, with many more victims of malnutrition and starvation as an indirect consequence of the fighting. Life expectancy is just 44 years, although this has increased from 40 years since 1975. In addition, there are thought to be over 50,000 orphaned children, and 50,000 people disabled as a result of the war. Over a million people have been displaced from their homes, some 300,000 of these to the neighbouring countries of Zaïre and Zambia. Despite these figures, however, population growth continues to be high: with a crude birth rate of 47 per thousand, population is growing annually by a high 2.6 per cent.

## Historical background

Historical development in sub-Saharan Africa is often (falsely) assumed to have begun with the arrival of Europeans in the region in the 15th century: in the case of Angola, for example, the country supposedly was 'discovered' in 1482 by the Portuguese explorer Diogo Cão, and much historical writing begins at this date. Such a perspective is not simply a result of Eurocentrism: it also reflects the fact that written historical sources are generally unavailable for before that time. Meanwhile, subsequent writing perhaps over-emphasizes the role of Europeans, not least because most documents used to reconstruct the history of this period were themselves written by European writers.

In one sense, this element of bias has been particularly significant in work on Angolan history. For example, much Portuguese writing during the colonial era, and a number of volumes in English by sympathizers with the Portuguese colonial régime, have pressed the argument that almost 500 years of unbroken influence was exercised by Portugal over 'its' colonies, including Angola. Although this viewpoint is much discredited, on the basis that for most of this time, there was little or no Portuguese presence in Angola, except as traders, and in some cases, missionaries, there is still a persuasive argument that Portuguese military and trading activities, and especially the slave trade, had a catastrophic effect on indigenous populations and societies.

However, in addition to this school of thought, there is also a considerable amount of writing on Angola which has focused not on the Portuguese impact on African societies, but on the internal evolution of those societies themselves, and indeed in some cases on the African influence on the Portuguese. This work has been based both on oral histories, and on the substantial archives relating to missionary activity, in particular in the Kongo kingdom which straddled the present-day countries of Angola, Zaïre, and the Congo Republic, and had its base in San Salvador, now M'banza Kongo, in northern Angola. The existence of this material, and the fact that for up to 400 years, Portuguese influence over the country was relatively slight, mean that the historical section of this bibliography has been divided not simply into 'pre-colonial' and 'colonial' history, but rather into sections dealing with the history of *African* kingdoms and societies up to the 19th century, and another dealing with *European* exploration, and the slave trade from 1483-1850.

Meanwhile, the section on 'colonial history' refers essentially to the period from the middle of the 19th century onwards. This reflects the fact that around this time, Portuguese interest in Africa took on a new shape. Previously concerned primarily with the development of trade, particularly in slaves, Portugal had been content to negotiate agreements with local rulers allowing this trade to continue. However, in the 19th century, all of the European powers began to seek territorial expansion in Africa. By the time of the Berlin Conference which carved up African territory between the European powers in 1884-85, Portugal was seeking to consolidate more or less direct rule over the whole Angolan territory, for the first time. Attempts also began to exploit the new colony's mineral and agricultural wealth, and by the time of the *Estado Novo*, established in Portugal in 1932 by the dictator Salazar, large numbers of Portuguese settlers had begun to arrive in a country now regarded as a 'province' of its 'mother' country.

Resistance to Portuguese rule was a constant theme in the late 19th and early 20th centuries, but this also took on a new form in 1961, as armed insurrection broke out, and a long guerilla struggle for independence began. As noted above, the three insurgent movements were associated to a certain extent with the major ethnic groupings of the country, although the MPLA, which was founded in 1956, has always had a much broader ethnic base than, for example, UNITA, founded in 1966 as a splinter group by the Ovimbundu leader, Jonas Savimbi. The FNLA meanwhile emerged from a previous organization, the *União das Populações do Norte de Angola*, which was founded in 1957, within the Bakongo population of the north.

Much more significant than ethnic differences, however, have been the contrasting ideologies and international backers of these different organizations. From an early stage, the MPLA developed close ties with communist organizations, and the Soviet Union, allying itself with other left-wing anti-colonial movements of the era. Savimbi's UNITA also adhered to communist ideology for a time, but within the Maoist camp (as did Holden Roberto and the FNLA). However, during the latter part of the independence struggle, it appears that links began to be established between UNITA and both the Portuguese and South African security forces. Certainly after independence, the links of UNITA with South Africa became plain, as it became pitched into full-scale conflict with the MPLA. The FNLA under Holden Roberto, meanwhile, was supported by the US in the immediate aftermath of independence, as a close ally of the Zaïrean President Mobutu. However, military defeat led to the US switching sides, to support UNITA as the only alternative to a Marxist government in Luanda.

## Angola since 1975

Independence itself was won not directly as a result of the armed struggle, but as a result of the Portuguese coup of April 25th, 1974, which placed in power in Lisbon a military government committed to decolonization. The period immediately after the coup saw the negotiation of the Alvor agreement, and the withdrawal of Portuguese troops. However, planned free democratic elections failed to take place, and as the situation deteriorated, over 300,000 Portuguese settlers fled, fearing for their future in an independent Angola.

Meanwhile, external factors continued to dominate the Angolan scene, as the country became the scene for superpower conflict: the MPLA became a model socialist ally for Moscow, whilst UNITA was seen as a last chance to stop the spread of communism in Africa by the US. The MPLA, bolstered by Soviet support and the presence of 15-20,000 Cuban troops, took power in Luanda in 1975. The leader of the MPLA, Agostinho Neto, became the country's first President, ruling until his death in 1979. After an unsuccessful coup attempt led by Nito Alves in May 1977, the party was also purged, transforming itself into a Marxist-Leninist party, the MPLA-PT (*Movimento Popular de Libertação de Angola-Partido de Trabalho*). Meanwhile, UNITA, deprived of power, continued its armed insurrection in the south of the country, taking control of many regional centres, and establishing an efficient army with direct support from the South African Defence Force (SADF). The stage was set for one of the most protracted and bloody civil wars of post-independence Africa.

A particularly fierce period of fighting occurred in the immediate post-independence period of 1975-76, known in Luanda as the 'Second War of Liberation'. During this period, the MPLA consolidated its power, forcing the temporary withdrawal of South African forces from the country, and inflicting a humiliating defeat on both South Africa and the US. However, low-level conflict continued, exacerbated in the 1980s by renewed military support for UNITA from the United States after the election of Ronald Reagan, and further direct intervention by South Africa. Since 1975, various attempts have been made to find a peaceful solution, but the external interests of the US, South Africa, the Soviet Union and Cuba mitigated against any real progress.

The first substantial breakthrough came with the signing of the New York accords of 1988, which established a linked settlement for Angola and neighbouring Namibia. The accords saw Cuban and South African troops withdraw from the country, as part of the process of initiating Namibian independence. Military events in 1987, which saw the failure of an Angolan/Cuban offensive on the UNITA-held town of Mavinga, followed by the failure of a counter attack on Cuito Cuanavale by UNITA and the South Africans, are now seen as crucial in persuading all sides that negotiation for an end to the conflict was the only viable solution. Although there was no immediate end to the war in Angola, the New York accords were followed by further developments, responding in particular to a thawing of East-West relations as communism collapsed in the former Soviet Union, as well as democratic changes in South Africa.

The first direct talks between the Angolan president, José Eduardo dos Santos, who took over from Agostinho Neto in 1979, and the UNITA leader, Jonas Savimbi, took place in June 1989, and within a year, a new peace effort had been launched by Portugal. By June 1991, both sides had signed the Bicesse peace accord, with the MPLA-PT agreeing to hold multi-party elections, whilst UNITA withdrew its own insistence on the establishment of a coalition government before elections were held. A ceasefire was established in May, and elections eventually set for September 1992. A Joint Political and Military Commission (CCPM) was established, with US, Soviet, and Portuguese observers, to oversee the peace process, whilst a Mixed Verification and Monitoring Commission (CMVF) was set up to monitor the ceasefire, with the assistance of 650 United Nations personnel. The ceasefire has not applied, however, to the oil-rich enclave of Cabinda, where the *Frente de Libertação do Enclave de Cabinda* (FLEC) continues to fight for independence.

Despite the signing of the peace accord, the political task facing Angola after sixteen years of civil war remained daunting. These included the demobilization of around 160,000 combatants from both sides, and their amalgamation into a new and much reduced army of 40,000 soldiers, as well as the holding of a census to register voters – an enormous task in such a vast and sparsely populated country, even without its recent history. Elections themselves passed relatively peacefully in September 1992, although at the time of writing their final outcome remained unclear. The MPLA, having abandoned its Marxist-Leninist credentials, polled just over 50 per cent of the votes, enabling it to form a new government, but its leader, José Eduardo dos Santos, failed to win the necessary majority to secure return to office as president. Prospects for peace thus remained dependent on the successful conclusion of a second round of polling for the presidency.

## The Angolan Economy

With continued uncertainty over political developments, and the devastating effect of almost thirty years of continuous war, the Angolan economy is unsurprisingly in a fairly poor condition, although prospects for an end to the war have led to some optimism. At the end of the colonial period, and despite armed rebellion since 1961, the Angolan economy had grown to a position where it was the fourth largest producer of coffee in the world, the fourth largest producer of diamonds, as well as a substantial oil and iron ore producer. There is some dispute as to the extent of 'development' in colonial Angola, and certainly a large part of the benefit of industrialization and mining growth that had occurred accrued only to a small section of the population.

However, on independence, the 1975/76 war led to a halt of production of iron ore, which has never been resumed, as well as severely curtailing diamond mining operations, as a result of UNITA attacks. Meanwhile, the exodus of Portuguese owners and managers, and nationalization of coffee plantations, followed by a withdrawal of the mainly Ovimbundu workforce of pickers, led to collapse of coffee production. The failure of the MPLA's policy of nationalizations, implemented in 1976, was compounded by damage done in particular to the country's infrastructure by the war. The country's three railways all ground to a halt at certain stages of the conflict, and the most significant, the Benguela railway, which runs through Zaire to the Copperbelt of Zambia, required major overhaul at the end of the 1980s after sustained attacks by UNITA.

The post-independence 'path' of the Angolan government was a socialist one, in which a fundamental transformation of society and the economy was attempted. However, in reality, this period was not to last long: by 1979, for example, rejection of foreign investment had been abandoned, and foreign companies began to be encouraged, particularly in the oil sector. Indeed, this sector has been the one success story of the post-independence Angolan economy. Oil had overtaken coffee as the major foreign exchange earner as early as 1973, but by 1991 it accounted for 89 per cent of exports, and 55 per cent of GDP. This growth in production has been overseen by partnership and joint venture agreements between the state and major foreign oil companies. Meanwhile, by 1985, the government had pulled away from nationalization in the agricultural sector too, moving instead to promote peasant production.

The latter part of the 1980s in Angola was characterized by attempts to rehabilitate the economy, and draw in foreign investment, reorientating government policy towards promotion of a limited free market. The country applied to join the World Bank and IMF, finally being accepted in 1988. In 1987, it implemented a structural adjustment package, the '*Saneamento Económico e Financeira*' (SEF, or Economic and Financial Restructuring), to curtail the money supply and promote economic recovery – on the IMF's terms. However, at the same time, foreign investment in certain sectors, such as education, health, and the media, remained prohibited, whilst a large public sector was maintained, in part because of the impossibility of reducing it prior to the elections.

One result of this new openness, particularly after the announcement of further economic reforms in the '*Programa de Acção do*

*Governo*' (Programme of Government Activity) in 1990, has been the growth of a huge speculative market in Angola. During 1991-92, South Africans farmers fearful of events in their own country began buying up cheap land in southern Angola, whilst, thousands of Portuguese settlers returned to reclaim their properties. In the manufacturing sector, bargain purchases of textile factories have been made by Asian companies seeking a new route to US or EC markets. With oil revenues rising as a result of the Gulf War, there was a huge surge in imports, and an increase in deals with western countries which swap aid, or loans, for oil. There is also a growing black market in gemstones, as diamond speculation and mining has been opened to the private sector. The lasting benefit of these changes to the Angolan economy remains to be seen.

## Culture and society

In addition to immense natural resources, Angola is also endowed with a rich cultural heritage, stretching from traditional sculpture, music, and dance, to modern poetry and prose writing. The MPLA in particular emerged as a party of the intelligentsia: the first Angolan President, Agostinho Neto, was a poet whose work was translated into several European languages during the liberation struggle, whilst writers and artists took posts as Ministers in the transitional government. After independence, an Angolan writers union was established, and this has been active in promoting cultural activity. A score of books by Angolan writers are easily available in Lisbon, although relatively few have been translated into English. In the main, Angolan literature is written in Portuguese, although some writers, such as José Luandino Vieira, attempt to reflect the vocabulary of the Luanda shanty towns by combining Portuguese and Kimbundu.

Alongside this more modern heritage, Angola also contains a vast store of local, traditional artists and customs. Particularly notable is the work and customs of the Chokwe and Lunda peoples of northeastern Angola, which is relatively well known as a result of extensive patronage of cultural studies by the former Belgian mining company, the *Companhia de Diamantes de Angola* (Diamang), in the diamond-mining area of Lunda province. A number of entries in this bibliography refer to joint publications of Diamang and the Dundo Museum of the same province; these, however, represent the tip of an iceberg of work, in that most Portuguese-language publications of the series have been excluded as relatively inaccessible to the English reader. Much is known too of Bakongo art, where Angolan members of this ethnic group share much in common culturally with peoples of the Congo Republic and Zaïre.

## Guide to the bibliography

This bibliography aims to provide coverage of a wide range of areas of Angolan history, politics, economy, society and culture, as well as the natural environment. However, the material contained within it does not provide a comprehensive account of Angola, for a number of reasons. For example, for detailed study, it is important to place material specifically on Angola included in this volume, in the context of the wider literature on southern Africa; there is also a wealth of material in Portuguese, much of it unavailable outside Angola or Portugal, which makes important reading. In compiling this bibliography, a number of decisions have been made both about what to include, and what to exclude, and in terms of order and convention.

First, the lack of correspondence between borders of African colonial and nation states on the one hand, and the ethnic and linguistic borders, or areas of influence of pre-colonial kingdoms on the other, causes some difficulty. For example, there is considerable ethnographic and linguistic material available for the Bakongo people, but for which fieldwork was carried out principally or exclusively in Zaïre or the Congo Republic; similarly, much material on peoples living in the east or south of the country actually involved fieldwork primarily in Namibia or Botswana, where members of the same ethnic groups live, with only occasional forays into Angola. As a general rule, material has only been included here where the work deals directly with communities living inside the borders of Angola. An attempt has been made nonetheless to include some directly relevant material from a neighbouring country where none is available for the Angolan side, and in these cases, the origin and focus of the work is clearly indicated. Meanwhile, in the historical case of the Kongo kingdom, which also straddled the border of modern states, material is generally included, except where it clearly refers only to events or places outside the boundaries of present-day Angola.

Another more intractable linguistic problem involves the relative shortage of material on Angola which is published in English. Much of the material which does exist, particularly on the economy or social conditions, is either rather old, or contained in recent, but unpublished or difficult to obtain reports for international organizations. In practice, older work has been included where it is either of historical interest on the colonial era, or there is no other suitable material available. Similarly, a small number of limited circulation reports have been included, particularly on current economic and social conditions. In addition, it has sometimes proved necessary to include some material in Portuguese, or in some cases in French, either to provide an adequate representation, or simply because of the importance of the source. This is especially true for work on some African languages spoken in Angola, and for certain historical and documentary material indispensable to a balanced view of early colonial history.

A third issue surrounds the massive variation in quality of books and articles on Angola, and indeed of those included in this volume. Most important, Angola is a country in which entrenched ideological positions have been part of political and literary reality for many years. On the independence struggle, and on post-independence conflict, material from both sides has been included, with commentaries attempting to resist approval or disapproval of any particular position. However, no author, or bibliography compiler, is ideologically neutral, and some allowance must be made for this in following up on material included.

In compiling this bibliography, considerable use has been made of the library of the School of Oriental and African Studies of the University of London; also King's College London has a large collection of work on Portugal and its former colonies, including material in Portuguese, whilst other material has been consulted, and is available in the British Library, and at the Bodleian Library at Oxford University. In Portugal, an essential source on both current research, and colonial materials, is the Documentation Centre of the *Centro de Informação e Difusão Amílcar Cabral* (CIDAC), in Lisbon (Rua Pinheiro Chagas). A large collection on Angola, though mainly in Portuguese, is also held by the *Biblioteca Nacional de Lisboa* (Campo Grande), whilst other useful libraries in Portugal include those of the *Sociedade de Geografia de Lisboa* (100, Rua das Portas de Santo Antão), and outside Lisbon, at the University of Coimbra, and the *Biblioteca Municipal do Porto*.

For the student of Angolan history, a number of more detailed archives are also available, although access to them is variable to say the least. In Luanda, archives include the *Arquivo Nacional de Angola*, as well as other more specialist archives created during the colonial era, although the current status of these is unclear. Similarly, in Portugal, most recent available reports suggest access to public and private archives is limited; of these, the most important would be the *Arquivo Histórico Ultramarino* (30, Calçada da Boa Hora, Lisbon), which contains much material on Portuguese settlement. In the US, various collections have material of interest. On missionary activity in Angola, there are extensive collections relating to the American Baptist

**Introduction**

Church (housed at the International Ministries Library, Valley Forge, Pennsylvania), the Methodist Board of Missions (in New York) and the American Board of Commissioners for Foreign Missions (housed at the Savery Library, Talladega College, Talladega, Alabama 35160). Material relating to American foreign policy in Angola during the independence period can be found in the Gerald R. Ford Library (1000 Beal Ave, Ann Arbor, Michigan 48109), particularly concerning Kissinger's travels in the region. Another useful source is, of course, the Library of Congress (Washington, DC 20540).

The entries which follow have been grouped into chapters according to their principal theme, with cross-references where an individual book or article covers two or more themes. Entries within each section are arranged alphabetically by the first non-article word of the title. Titles are spelt as they are in the original work. However, in the annotations that accompany each entry, place and personal names are cited according to the spelling of the *Times Atlas*, which in most cases follows Portuguese convention.

*Acknowledgements*

Various people have been of assistance in the preparation of this volume. Thanks are due to Marga Holness, Simon Hunt, Patrick Chabal and others for pointing me in the right direction for a number of works included. Much of the research was carried out in the library of the School of Oriental and African Studies in London, and at the *Centro de Informação e Difusão Amílcar Cabral* in Lisbon, whose staff have been most helpful. Thanks also to Roma Beaumont and Gordon Reynell for continuing cartographic assistance. Naturally, the errors remain my own.

# Glossary

| | |
|---|---|
| **BOSS** | Bureau of Security Services (South Africa) |
| **CCPM** | Joint Political and Military Commission |
| **CIDAC** | Centro de Informação e Difusão Amílcar Cabral (Lisbon) |
| **CMVF** | Mixed Verification and Monitoring Commission |
| **FDA** | Forum Democrático Angolano |
| **FLEC** | Frente para a Libertação do Enclave de Cabinda |
| **FNLA** | Frente Nacional de Libertação de Angola |
| **Frelimo** | Frente de Libertação de Moçambique |
| **IICT** | Instituto de Investigação Científica Tropical (Lisbon) |
| **KZA** | Holland Committee on Southern Africa (Netherlands) |
| **MPLA** | Movimento Popular de Libertação de Angola |
| **MPLA-PT** | Movimento Popular de Libertação de Angola – Partido de Trabalho |
| **PAIGC** | Partido Africano de Independência do Guiné e do Cabo Verde (Guinea-Bissau) |
| **PIDE** | Polícia Internal de Defesa do Estado (Portugal pre-1975) |
| **PRA** | People's Republic of Angola |
| **PRD** | Partido Renovador Democrático |
| **SADF** | South African Defence Force |
| **SEF** | Saneamento Económica e Financeira |
| **SWAPO** | South West African Peoples' Organization (Namibia) |
| **UNDP** | United Nations Development Programme |
| **UNDRO** | United Nations Disaster Relief Organization |
| **UNECA** | United Nations Economic Commission for Africa |
| **UNIDO** | United Nations Industrial Development Organization |
| **UNITA** | União Nacional de Independência Total de Angola |
| **UNRISD** | United Nations Research Institute for Social Development |
| **UNTA** | União Nacional dos Trabalhadores de Angola |
| **UPA** | União das Populações de Angola |
| **UPNA** | União dos Povos do Norte de Angola |

# Theses and Dissertations on Angola

Manuela M. Palmerim. The sterile mother: aspects of court symbolism among the Lunda of Mwant Yaav (Aruund). MPhil thesis, London School of Economics, 1986.

Robert Joseph Papstein. The upper Zambezi: a history of the Luvale people, 1000-1900. PhD thesis, University of California, Los Angeles, 1978. 302p.

Anne Wilson. The Kongo kingdom to the mid-seventeenth century. PhD thesis, University of London, 1977.

Douglas L. Wheeler. The Portuguese in Angola, 1836-1891: a study in expansion and administration. PhD thesis, Boston University, Massachussetts, 1963. 442p.

Alvin Willard Urquhart. Patterns of settlement and subsistence in southwestern Angola. PhD thesis, University of California, Berkeley, 1962. 149p.

John Erni Remick. American influence on the education of the Ovimbundu (the Benguela and Bié highlands) of Angola, Africa, from 1880-1914. PhD thesis, Miami University. 132p.

Harry W. Nerhood. The proposed distribution of the Portuguese colonies between 1898 and 1914. PhD thesis, Ohio State University, Columbus, Ohio, 1946. 847p.

Donald Francis Heisel. The indigenous populations of the Portuguese African territories. PhD thesis, University of Wisconsin, Madison, 1966. 220p.

Siad Yusuf Abdi. Racial belief systems of nationalist movements. A case study of Angola and South Africa. PhD thesis, University of Denver, Colorado, 1989. 400p.

Mark S. C. Simpson. The Soviet Union and Afro-Marxist regimes: the path to treaties of friendship and cooperation. PhD thesis, London School of Economics, 1989. 400p.

# The Country and Its People

1 **Angola: Portuguese province in Africa.**
Angola Institute (Instituto de Angola).   Luanda: Publicações Unidade,
1953. 207p. maps.
Provides an introduction to the geography, geology, climate and population of colonial
Angola, before discussing issues such as colonial administration, public health,
education, production, transport and communications, foreign trade, and finance. It
includes numerous statistical tables, diagrams, photographs, and some colour
reproductions of paintings, although the text is little more than propaganda.

2 **Area handbook for Angola.**
Allison Butler Herrick (et al.).   Washington, DC: American University
Press, 1967. 439p. maps. bibliog. (Foreign Area Studies).
One of a series of handbooks, this work outlines the historical background of Angola
and then presents information about the colony, divided into sections on social,
economic, political, and military issues. Although it deals only with the period up to
1966, this is still a standard reference work on the colonial period, providing a
comprehensive survey of the economy and society. An extensive bibliography and
glossary is also included.

3 **Les angolais.** (The Angolans.)
Robert Davezies.   Paris: Editions des Minuit, 1965. 259p. (Grands
Documents, no. 25).
A collection of essays by and about prominent Angolans in the 1960s. The book
includes interviews, and facts and figures about Angola, as well as the Portuguese
influence on the region.

4 **A few words about Angola.**

A. C. Valdes Thomaz dos Santos.   Luanda: Governo Geral de Angola, Direcção dos Serviços de Economia, 1948. 33p.

A brief description of colonial Angola, including its administration, education system, production and commerce, published by the Portuguese government for external consumption.

5 **Portugal's overseas provinces: facts and figures.**

Lisbon: Agência-Geral do Ultramar, [n.d.]. 177p. maps.

This booklet, produced in the 1960s, includes information on the geography, relief, hydrology, climate and population of each of the Portuguese colonies, followed by a description of the main towns, a brief history, and an outline of colonial administration.

6 **Portuguese Africa: a handbook.**

Edited by David M. Abshire, Michael A. Samuels.   New York: Praeger; London: Pall Mall, 1969. 480p. maps.

An important general text for all of Portuguese Africa before independence, which includes substantial sections, though no separate chapters, on Angola. This work covers the physical, political and social background to the territories, as well as aspects of the government, economy, and the country's position in the international political economy. It also includes numerous maps and statistics.

# Geography and Geology

## General

7 **O clima de Angola.** (The climate of Angola.)
Luanda: Serviço Meteorológico de Angola, 1955. 53p. maps.
A description of the climate of Angola, supplemented by a number of useful statistical tables and maps.

8 **Contribution to the geology of Benguella.**
J. W. Gregory. *Transactions, Royal Society of Edinburgh*, vol. 51, no. 3 (1917), p. 495-536.
A description of the geology of Benguela province in southern Angola, based on the author's travels in the area in 1912. This issue of the Transactions also contains articles by other authors which deal specifically with the petrography of Benguela, (p. 537-60); cretaceous brachiopods and molluscs (p. 561-80); algal limestone (p. 581-84) and cretaceous echinoids (p. 585-87), but all are based on analysis of rock specimens brought back from Angola to Edinburgh by Gregory.

9 **The Damara system in Angola: some preliminary observations on the existence of two geosyncline facies.**
Joaquim Raul Torquato. Luanda: Instituto de Investigação Científica de Luanda, 1971. 27p. bibliog. map. (Relatórios e Communicações, no. 13).
Contains a description of the Damara geological system of southwestern Angola, near the mouth of the Cunene River. The text is in English and Portugese; and a number of colour photographs are also included.

10    **Geographic provinces of Angola: an outline based on recent sources.**
      D. S. Whittlesey.    *Geographical Review*, vol. 14 (Jan. 1924), p. 113-26.
This is an early description of the geography of Angola, including relief, climate and hydrography. Detailed descriptions are provided of the coastal and highland areas around Benguela, Luanda and Moçamedes (now Namibe), as well as the southern desert, the Upper Zambesi valley, and the Congo border.

11    **Notes on the Kunene river, southern Angola.**
      F. E. Kanthack.    *Geographical Journal*, vol. 57, no. 5 (May 1921), p. 321-36.
Presents a description of the climate and physical geography of the area along the Cunene river and the border between Angola and what is now Namibia including maps, photographs and tables of rainfall and river discharge. The author visited the area to resolve a boundary dispute between the Portuguese and British governments, and the final part of the article provides a review of this dispute.

12    **O relevo do sudoeste de Angola: estudo de geomorfologia.** (The relief of southwest Angola: a geomorphological study.)
      Mariano Feio.    Lisbon: Junta de Investigação Científica do Ultramar, 1981. 326p. maps. bibliog. (Memórias da Junta de Investigação Científica do Ultramar, no. 67).
A description of the geomorphology of southeast Angola, dealing separately with the main plateau area, the Cuanhame basin, the course of the Cunene river, the southern deserts and the Otchinjau-Oncócua region. There are also observations on sedimentary geology and structures, and present-day erosional processes. A ten page English summary is appended.

13    **Southern Africa: a geographical study. Volume 1: Physical geography.**
      John H. Wellington.    Cambridge, England: Cambridge University Press, 1955. 528p.
This volume, unlike its sister volume on social and economic geography, retains some relevance in spite of its date, both in the form of maps, and descriptions of geological and geomorphological structures, climate, vegetation, soils and hydrography.

**Ensaio de um estudo geográfico da rede urbana de Angola.** (Analysis of a geographical study of the urban network of Angola.)
*See* item no. 436

**Luanda e os seus 'muceques': problemas de geografia urbana.** (Luanda and its Shanties: problems of urban geography.)
*See* item no. 438

**Outlines of wildlife conservation in Angola.**
*See* item no. 439

**Boletim da Sociedade de Geografia de Lisboa.** (Bulletin of the geographical society of Lisbon.)
*See* item no. 535

**Bibliografia geológica do ultramar português.** (Geological bibliography of the Portuguese overseas territories.)
*See* item no. 555

# Maps and atlases

14 **Angola: Official standard names approved by the US Board on Geographic Names.**
Washington, DC: Office of Geography, Department of the Interior, 1956. 234p. (Gazetteer, no. 20).
Provides a list of standard place names in Angola, with designation, latitude and longitude, area, and a reference to one of six maps of the country. Other non-standard names are cross referenced to those 'approved' by the board.

15 **Benguella railway: plan and profile of the railway from Lobito Bay to Kambove.**
London: Sir Douglas Fox & Partners, Sir Charles Metcalfe, Engineers, 1914. map. Scale 1:400,000.
An early map of the Benguela railway from the coast in Angola through to the copperbelt of Zambia, with vertical and horizontal profiles.

16 **Carta de Angola.** (Map of Angola.)
Lisbon: Junta das Missões Geográficas e de Investigações do Ultramar, 1958-64. 4 maps. Scale: 1:1,000,000.
Mapmaking in Angola reflects external influence more than any other sector. These four colonial maps provide good coverage of Angola; subsequent, larger scale maps were also produced by the CIA in 1970 (Scale 1:3,250,000) and by the Soviet authorities (Scale 1:2,500,000).

17 **Carta fitogeográfica de Angola.** (Phytogeographic map of Angola.)
L. A. G. Barbosa. Luanda: Instituto de Investigação Científica de Angola, 1970. 323p.
Contains a basic vegetation map of Angola, with a detailed accompanying description of each phytogeographic zone. An earlier map with the same name was produced in 1939 by John Gosseweiler (Lisbon: República Portuguesa, Ministério das Colónias. 236p.). Both maps contain a full index of plant species.

18 **Carta geológica de Angola.** (Geological map of Angola.)
Lisbon: Direcção Provincial dos Serviços de Geologia e Minas, 1971. maps. Scale: 1:100,000.
This series of geological maps achieved incomplete coverage of the country, although the diamond mining province of Lunda Norte, and the area around Benguela, are relatively well covered. Another series of larger scale geological maps (1:250,000) began production in 1972, starting with the same two areas. Both series were interrupted by the departure of the Portuguese from Angola.

19   **Carta geral dos solos de Angola.** (Generalized soil map of Angola.)
    Missao de Pedologia de Angola e Moçambique.   Lisbon: Junta de
    Investigações do Ultramar, 1959-72. 6 vols. maps. bibliog.
    (Memórias da Junta de Investigações do Ultramar, 2nd series, nos. 9 [Huíla], 27
    [Huambo], 45 [Moçamedes], 57 [Cabinda], 63 [Uíge and Zaïre], and 65
    [Benguela]).
    These soil maps at a scale of 1:1,000,000 were prepared at provincial level. Each is
    presented alongside a description (in Portuguese) of each soil type and its
    accompanying vegetation, climate and topography. Each also contains an extensive
    bibliography on the soils of Angola, which extends to over 230 entries in the most
    recent volume.

20   **Generalized soil map of Angola.**
    J. V. Botelho da Costa, Ario de Azevedo.   Madison, Wisconsin: 7th
    International Congress of Soil Science, 1960, p. 56-62.
    A soil map of Angola, with commentary in English. The latter includes discussion of
    parent materials, and the occurrence of laterites, as well as salinized and/or alkalized
    soils. A revised version of the map, with text in Portuguese, was published as '*Carta
    generalizada dos solos de Angola, 3ª aprox.*' (*Memórias da Junta de Investigação do
    Ultramar*, 2nd series, vol. 56 (1968) p. 1-277).

21   **Planta de Luanda, com o plano de urbanização e roteiro.** (Plan of
    Luanda, with the urbanization scheme, and guide.)
    Luanda: Imprensa Nacional da Colónia de Angola, 1944. 35p. map.
    A town plan of Luanda in the 1940s, which is of interest since it superimposes a sketch
    of proposed new roads and developments. The guide also includes a road index, with
    directions of how to find each road.

**The rose-coloured map. Portugal's attempt to build an African empire from
the Atlantic to the Indian Ocean.**
*See* item no. 123.


# Tourist and travel guides

22   **Africa on a shoestring.**
    Geoff Crowther.   London: Lonely Planet, 1985. 4th ed. 752p. maps.
    This relatively up-to-date travel guide includes just five pages on Angola, providing a
    brief history of the country, details of how to obtain a visa, and a very short description
    of available hotel accommodation in Luanda.

23 **Angola.**
Frederic Pedro Marjay. Lisbon: Livraria Bertrand, 1961. [n.p.] maps.
(Colecção Romántica, no. 10).
A coffee-table travel book in A4 format, including text in Portuguese and English. It provides a travelogue of journeys from Luanda to Dundo in the northeast, the Cabinda enclave, and along the coast to Benguela, Moçamedes (now Namibe), and Baía dos Tigres in the south. Much of the book consists of photos, some in colour, that portray the cities, people and landscapes of Angola under Portuguese rule.

24 **Guia roteiro turístico de Angola.** (A tourist's travel guide to Angola.)
Luanda: Angolana, 1967/68. maps.
Despite its Portuguese title, this is an English-language guide to the province of Angola, with a description of its historical and economic development, followed by detailed information on tourist sites, hotels, night clubs, shopping, safaris and touring. Individual sections cover each of the 15 districts in more detail.

# Early travellers' accounts

25 **Angola and the River Congo.**
Joachim John Monteiro. London: Frank Cass, 1968. 2nd ed. 2 vols.
maps. bibliog. (Cass Library of African Studies, no. 43).
Based on travels by the author, this work provides an account of visits to various regions of the country. Volume 1 covers the coastal zone from the river Congo south to Ambriz, including the inland towns of Bembe and San Salvador (now M'Banza Kongo); volume 2 covers the towns of Luanda, Benguela, and Moçamedes (now Namibe), including the valleys of the rivers Zenza and Cuanza. For each area, the local economy, customs and artefacts are described, interspersed by comments on the work of missionaries and the colonial authorities, accounts of local flora and fauna, native remedies, and local cooking, as well as tales recounted to the author during his journey. A brief history is included, translated from an earlier work in Portuguese by Feo Cardozo, along with a description of the physical geography and geology of the area as a whole, and a vigorous defence of the slave trade.

26 **Angolan sketches.**
T. Alexander Barns. London: Methuen, 1928. 206p. maps.
This is a travelogue and early regional geography of colonial Angola, dealing separately with the central, northern and southern regions of the colony, and including observations on climate, health, farming, sport and adventure. Includes advice on hunting gorillas, and emphasizes the importance of road and rail travel in opening up the interior to development.

27 **From Benguella to the territory of Yacca: description of a journey into Central and West Africa.**
H. Capello, R. Ivens, translated from the Portuguese by Alfred Elwes.
London: Sampson, Low, Marston, Searle & Rivington, 1882. 2 vols. maps.

A description of the journey by the authors, two Portuguese naval captains, along the Cuanza River (volume 1), and then north to the Cuango on the border between present day Angola and Zaïre (volume 2). Each volume contains detailed observations of the people and environment of the areas visited, as well as surveys of the Cunene, Cubango, Luando, Cuanza and Cuango rivers. A number of appendices at the end of the second volume include detailed tables of geographical observations; notes on fauna; an extensive Portuguese-Umbundu-English vocabulary; and shorter comparable vocabularies for N'Jenji, Garanganja, Chokwe, Lunda and Ca-Luiana.

28 **A fossiker in Angola.**
(Captain) Malcolm Burr.   London: Figurehead, 1933. 204p. maps.

An account of Burr's journey to the district of Moxico, which includes descriptions of the peoples he encountered, as well as of fauna and flora, and general comments on the area. There is also a preface by Henry Nevinson.

29 **Garanenze, or seven years pioneer mission work in Central Africa.**
Frederick Stanley Arnot.   London: Frank Cass, 1969. 2nd ed. 271p. maps.

The diary of missionary and explorer Arnot, during his travels in central Africa in 1881-88. Chapters 3 and 4 of the book cover the part of the journey spent in Angola on the Benguela plateau, and on the west coast. This new edition has an introduction by Robert I. Rotberg. The original was published by Frank Cass of London in 1889.

30 **How I crossed Africa, from the Atlantic to the Indian Ocean, through unknown countries: discovery of the great Zambezi affluents. Volume 1: The king's rifle. Volume 2: The Coillard family.**
(Major) Alexandre de Serpa Pinto, translated from the Portuguese by Alfred Elwes.   London: Sampson Low, Marston, Searle, & Rivington, 1881. 2 vols. maps.

A description of the important Serpa Pinto expedition of 1877, in which the author attempted to stake a claim for Portuguese sovereignty across central Africa from Angola to Mozambique. Volume 1 deals mainly with the time spent in what is now Angola, covering the journey from Benguela to Bié, and then east, across the Cuanza river, to the territory of the Luchazi and the Mbwela. Various Portuguese newspapers of the time containing articles relating to this expedition, and the consequent dispute between England and Portugal, are available at the National Newspaper Library, Hendon, England.

31 **Journey in Africa through Angola, Ovampoland and Damaraland.**
Peter A. Möller, translated from the Swedish and annotated by Ione and
Jalmar Rudner. Cape Town: R. Struik, 1974. 216p. maps. bibliog.

This translation of Captain Möller's travels in southern Angola and Namibia
(originally published in Stockholm as *Resa i Afrika genom Angola, Ovampo und
Damaraland*, 1899) provides a wealth of first-hand information on native peoples, the
Angola (Dorsland) trekkers, and wildlife. It is supplemented by additional notes by the
translators at the end of the book, and an updated map.

32 **The lands of the Cazembe: Lacerda's journey to Cazembe in 1798.**
F. J. M. de Lacerda e Almeida, translated from the Portuguese and
annotated by Captain R. F. Burton, KCMG. London: John Murray,
1873. 271p. maps.

This edition of the travels of the Portuguese explorer Lacerda contains his account of
his own expeditions into central Africa, and of the subsequent journey of the
*pombeiros*, P. J. Baptista and Amaro José, from Angola to Tete in Mozambique
(translated from the Portuguese by B. A. Beadle). Also included is a resumé of
Monteiro and Gamitto's travels from Portuguese East Africa to the Cazembe kingdom
(written by Charles Beke). The volume was published under the auspices of the Royal
Geographical Society in London.

33 **Narrative of an expedition to explore the River Zaïre.**
(Captain) J. K. Tuckey. London: Frank Cass, 1967. 498p.

An account of the ill-fated journey of Captain Tuckey, a classic of exploration texts,
first published in 1818. Along with the journal of Professor Smith (q.v.), the book
provides a description of Cabinda, and the southern, Angolan, bank of the River
Zaïre, including considerable botanical information.

34 **Narrative of the voyages to explore the shores of Africa, Arabia and
Madagascar.**
(Captain) W. F. W. Owen. Farnborough, England: Gregg
International, 1968. 2 vols.

The voyages of Owen revolutionized understanding of the hydrography of the African
coast. The first of these volumes includes many observations on Angola.

35 **The other Livingstone.**
Judith Listowel. London: Julian Friedmann, 1974. 312p. maps. bibliog.

An account of the travels of the little known Hungarian explorer, László Magyar
(1818-68), who Listowel describes, along with William Oswell (1818-93) and Cândido
Cardoso (1805-80) as 'Livingstone's helpers'. Magyar travelled through much of central
and southern Angola.

36 **Reality versus romance in south central Africa.**
James Johnston. London: Frank Cass, 1969. 2nd ed. 353p. maps.

This relatively little-known account of the author's expedition across Africa, which
started in Angola in May 1891, and ended in Mozambique in October of the following
year, is of interest since it paints a picture somewhat at variance with other missionary

and expedition accounts of the time. One of Johnston's purposes on this trip was to demonstrate the suitability of West Indians for manual labour in tropical Africa. This aside, his conciliatory, rather than confrontational attitude to local people is striking, as is his contempt for much missionary activity. Although only the first five chapters of the book deal with present day Angola, Johnston does single out the eastern highlands of the country as an area suitable for future missions. As a medical doctor, he also makes some interesting comments on sanitary conditions in Benguela.

37   **Six years of a traveller's life in Western Africa.**
Francisco Travassos Valdez.   London: Hurst & Blackett, 1861. 2 vols.

An account of the author's travels along the west coast of Africa. Volume 2 covers his journeys along the coast of Angola, through Luanda to Benguela and Moçamedes (now Namibe). There are numerous observations on the history, customs and artefacts of the people he encountered, as well as descriptions of economic and political life. Inland areas are also described, largely on the basis of other Portuguese sources. The author argues that exploitation of copper reserves, and the potential for cotton cultivation, far outweigh the economic argument for continuance of the slave trade.

38   **Through Angola: a coming colony.**
(Colonel) John C. B. Statham.   Edinburgh, London: William Blackwood & Sons, 1922. 388p. maps. bibliog.

This work is in two parts, the first an account of a hunting trip to Angola, and the second a general commentary on the geography, history and customs of the colony. Both draw on the author's diary, and the latter also on historical sources. Also included are observations on a number of animals, an index of flora, and notes on the 'physiography and climate (which) may help the traveller in Angola to avoid unhealthy regions and seasons' (p. vii).

39   **Through unknown Africa: experiences from the Jaspert African Expedition of 1926-27.**
Willem Jaspert, translated from the German by Agnes Platt.   London: Jarrolds, 1930. 288p. maps.

This is the diary of Willem Jaspert's expedition from Benguela along the line of rail in Moxico district, and the town of Vila Luso (now Luena).

40   **Two trips to Gorilla Land and the cataracts of the Congo.**
Richard Burton.   New York: Johnson Reprint, 1967. 2 vols.

These are notes from the voyages in 1861-63 by Burton, a British Consul, along the Gabon coast, to the Congo river, and through parts of northern Angola. This work was first published in 1876.

41   **Visit to the Portuguese possessions in south-western Africa.**
Georg Tams, translated from the German, and with an introduction and annotations by H. Evans Lloyd.   London: T. C. Newby, 1845. 2 vols.

An account of the travels in Angola of the German physician Georg Tams. In addition to describing the physical appearance of the land, its natural resources, and the customs and traditions of the African population, the book gives an account of the slave trade operating out of ports from Ambriz in the north, to Novo Redondo (now

Sumbe) in the south. The author also gives a detailed account of the 'Negro kingdom of Ambriz'.

42    **Wild bush tribes of tropical Africa: an account of adventure and travel amonst pagan people in tropical Africa, with a description of their manners of life, customs, heathenish rites and ceremonies, secret societies, sport and warfare, collected during a sojourn of twelve years.**
      C. Cyril Claridge.    London: Seeley, Service & Co., 1922. 309p. maps.
An amateur ethnography of the Bakongo of northern Angola, based on the author's travels around the town of San Salvador (now M'Banza Kongo). It focuses on discussion of religious and magical practices, or 'fetishes', as well as other issues mentioned in the subtitle.

**Report on the work of the commission sent out by the Jewish Territorial Organization under the auspices of the Portuguese government to examine the territory proposed for the purpose of a Jewish settlement in Angola.**
*See* item no. 180.

# Flora and Fauna

43   **The Benguela and comparable ecosystem.**
Edited by A. I. L. Payne, J. A. Gulland, K. H. Brink.   Cape Town:
RSA Department of Environment Affairs, Sea Fisheries Research Unit,
1987. 957p. (South African Journal of Marine Science, vol. 5).

A collection of some sixty-nine papers on the ecology of the Benguela Upwelling
Region off the coast of southern Angola and Namibia. The papers cover hydrodynamic
influences on plant and animal communities in the sea, biological interactions, whole
system ecology and implications for fishing. Although much of the information is of
relevance to Angolan waters, the papers themselves are dominated by the work of
South African scientists off the coast of Namibia and South Africa.

44   **Biogeography and ecology of southern Africa.**
Edited by M. J. A. Werger.   The Hague: Junk, 1978. 2 vols. maps.

The reader interested in the biogeography and ecology of Angola will have to search in
this volume for relevant information, which is organized by phyto- and zoogeograph-
ical zones, rather than by country. Chapter 9, for example, covers the Karoo-Namib
region which touches southern Angola, whilst Chapter 10 which focuses on the
Sudano-Zambezian region covers the Central Highlands. Nonetheless, this is an
invaluable and comprehensive account of the biogeography of the region, with detailed
descriptions of habitats, and extensive references.

45   **Catalogue of the African plants collected by Dr Friedrich Welwitsch in
1853-1861.**
William Philip Hiern, (et al.).   London: British Museum, Department
of Botany, 1896-1901. 6 vols. bibliog.

A catalogue of part of a collection of over 5,000 species of plants collected by Dr
Welwitsch, a German botanist working for the Portuguese government, which
remained in the Natural History Museum in London after his death. The first four
parts, arranged by Hiern, and published from 1896-1900, cover the dicotyledons. Two

further volumes deal with the monocotyledons and gymnosperms (arranged by Alfred Barton Rendle, and published in 1899), and the cryptogamia (arranged by various authors, and published in 1901). The main study collection was moved to Lisbon after a legal contest over ownership.

46 **Checklist of Angolan birds.**
M. A. Traylor. Lisbon: Companhia de Diamantes de Angola (Diamang), 1963. 250p. (Publicações Culturais, no. 61).
A standard reference work on Angolan birds.

47 **Conspectus florae Angolensis.** (Guide to Angolan flora.)
Edited by Luis Wittnich Carrisso. Lisbon: Junta de Investigações do Ultramar, 1937-82. 9 vols.
This series provides a detailed description, in Portuguese, of the plants of Angola. Individual volumes cover the Ranunculaceae and Malvaceae (vol. 1 no. 1 [1937]); the Malvaceae and Aquifoliaceae (vol. 1, no. 2 [1951]); the Celastraceae and Connaracea (vol. 2, no. 1 [1954]) and the Leguminosae (vol. 2, no. 2 [1956]; vol. 3, no. 1 [1962]; and vol. 3, no. 2 [1966]), all compiled by A. W. Exell and F. A. Mendonça. Volume 4, by A. W. Exell, A. Fernandes and E. J. Mendes then covers the Rosaceae and the Alangiaceae (1970); volume 5, by E.A.C.L.E. Schelpe deals with the Pteridophyta (1977), whilst volume 6, by Rosette Fernandes, covers the Carassulaceae (1982). The series was elaborated by the Botanic Institute of the University of Coimbra in Portugal, in collaboration with the British Museum, London.

48 **Lista dos insectos com interesse económico em Angola.** (List of insects of economic importance in Angola.)
A. P. S. Fonseca Ferrão, Helder A. R. A. Leite Cardoso. Nova Lisboa (Chianga), Angola: VI Jornadas Silvo-Agronómicas, 1965. 39p. bibliog.
Contains two lists of insects, the first arranged by hosts, and their respective parasites, and the second by insect, divided into pests and parasites. Incorporated in the former is an indication of the economic importance of the insect for different crops. Latin names of all insects are provided.

49 **Nomes indígenas de plantas de Angola.** (Indigenous names of Angolan plants.)
John Gosseweiler. Luanda: Imprensa Nacional, 1953. 587p. maps.
The first part of the book consists of a comprehensive list of indigenous names for plants, each with the Latin name, the locality in which it is found, the name of the collector who first identified it, and the language from which the name originates. Part two then provides a full description of each species in Portuguese, and an index of botanical names.

50  **Plantas úteis da Africa portuguesa.** (Useful plants of Portuguese Africa.)
F. de Mello de Ficalho, edited by Ruy Telles Palhina.  Lisbon: Agência
Geral das Colónias, 1947. 2nd ed. 301p.

First published in 1884, this guide includes a short history of cultivated plants in Africa,
and then provides details of various botanical expeditions, with a description of the
medical, culinary and other uses of plants discovered.

51  **Research on the mosquitoes of Angola (*Diptera, Culicidae*) X – the gems
*Culex*, L., 1758. Checklist with new records, keys to females and larvae,
distribution, taxonomic and bioecological notes.**
H. Ribeiro, Helena da Cunha Ramos.  Lisbon: Junta de Investigações
Científicas do Ultramar, 1980. 175p. bibliog. (Estudos, Ensaios,
Documentos, no. 134).

A description of mosquitoes in Angola.

52  **A statistical analysis of a sample of the flora of Angola.**
A. W. Exell, M. L. Gonçalves. *Garcia de Orta, Series Botánica,* vol. 1
(1973), p. 105-28.

A short article describing a sample of flora from southern Angola.

53  **The vegetation of Angola.**
E. K. Airy Shaw.  *Journal of Ecology,* vol. 35 (1947), p. 23-48.

A précis of J. Gosseweiler and F.A. Mendonça's classic monograph (*Carta
fitogeográfica de Angola,* [1939]), which describes the vegetation of the country divided
into nine sub-regions, according to Rübel's classification system. They range from rain
forest in the north, to desert in the south, although two, the rain forest, and 'montane
woody communities' cover 80 per cent of the land area of the country. A useful
glossary of vernacular plant names is also included.

# Prehistory and Archaeology

**54  An archaeological reconnaissance tour of Angola.**
J. Rudner. *South African Archaeological Bulletin*, vol. 31, nos. 123-24 (Dec. 1976), p. 99-111.
A report of a visit to Angola by the author in 1971, which makes special reference to Strandloper remains, and to rock art. Nine sites of prehistoric rock art in central and southern Angola are described in turn.

**55  Arqueologia angolana.** (Angolan archaeology.)
Carlos Ervedosa.  Lisbon: Edições 70, 1980. 444p. maps. bibliog.
A full treatment of the archaeology of Angola, which starts with a discussion of the Stone and Iron Ages in Africa as a whole. After this introduction, the archaeology of Angola is presented in three parts. In part 1, pre-historic cultures are described for each ecological zone, focusing in particular on the northeast of the country. The geomorphology and quarternary stratigraphy of each area are also outlined, and a reconstruction made of their cultural history. Part 2 deals with rock art, providing a description of twenty-two different locations of significance. Finally, in part 3, megalithic constructions are described, including fortifications and tumuli. Each section is well-illustrated with photographs, and in the case of part 2, numerous sketches and drawings of symbols found carved into the rock. This is an essential guide.

**56  The distribution of prehistoric culture in Angola.**
J. Desmond Clark.  Lisbon: Companhia de Diamantes de Angola (Diamang), 1966. 102p. maps. bibliog. (Museu do Dundo, Publicações Culturais, no. 23).
Describes artefacts from throughout the Stone Age found in various parts of Angola. Three zones are distinguished: the Congo zone in the north; the Zambezi zone in the southeast, and the southwest zone. Individual pieces are placed in the context of the stratigraphy in which they were found. Another publication by the author in the same series focuses on pre-historic culture in northeast Angola (*Pre-historic cultures of*

15

*northeast Angola and their significance in tropical Africa.* Lisbon: Diamang, 1963. [Publicações Culturais do Museo do Dundo, no. 62]).

57 **Leba. Estudos do quaternário, pré-história e arqueologia.** (Leba. Studies of the quaternary, pre-history and archaeology.)
Lisbon: Instituto de Investigaáão Científica Tropical, Centro de Pré-História e Arqueologia, 1978- . occasional.

An occasional journal publishing work on the pre-history and archaeology of Africa, with special reference to Portuguese-speaking countries. The studies are mainly in Portuguese, but do include some contributions in other European languages. Each volume includes a summary of each article in English.

58 **Pleistocene climates and cultures in north-eastern Angola.**
E. M. van Zinderen Bakker, J. Desmond Clark. *Nature,* vol. 196 (Nov. 1962), p. 639-42.

This article presents radiocarbon dates for pollen samples taken from the Lunda region of northeast Angola, to support evidence of Pleistocene climatic change previously inferred from elsewhere in central and southern Africa. It also includes a brief description of the geography of the Lunda region.

59 **The stone age archaeology of southern Africa.**
C. Garth Sampson. London, New York: Academic, 1974. 518p. maps. bibliog.

A major text on the archaeology of southern Africa, which includes Angola. There are a number of references to excavations in northwestern Angola, and these are placed in the context of finds elsewhere in the region. As a whole, the book aimed to revise the framework for analysis of Stone Age archaeology in the region. In the context of Angola, the book synthesises available material, although it is based mainly on the work of J. Desmond Clark (q.v.).

60 **Tentative study of the pleistocene climatic changes and stone age culture sequence in north-eastern Angola.**
L. S. B. Leakey. Luanda: Companhia de Diamantes de Angola (Diamang), 1949. 82p. maps. (Museo do Dundo, Subsídios para a História, Arqueologia e Etnografia da Lunda, Publicações Culturais no. 4).

Based on a three week visit to the Lunda area of northeast Angola with J. Janmart, this study presents archaeological evidence for substantial pleistocene climatic change, including a series of glacial and interglacial periods, which the author links with European glacial episodes. Sequences of culture are also inferred, from a variety of implements excavated from this diamond-rich area. Correlations are made between these sequences, and those previously found across central Africa to Uganda and Kenya. Janmart himself also published a study in the same series, entitled *The Kalahari sands of the Lunda (NSE), their earlier redistributions, and the Sangoan culture* (Lisbon: Diamang, 1953. [Publicações Culturais do Museu do Dundo, no. 20]).

**Contribuição para uma bibliografia sobre o quaternário e pré-história de Angola.** (Contribution to a bibliography on the Quaternary and pre-history of Angola.)
*See* item no. 559.

# History

## General

61 **Angola.**
Douglas L. Wheeler, René Pélissier. London: Greenwood, 1978. 2nd
ed. 296p. bibliog.
An authoritative but readable introduction to Angolan society and history in the
colonial era. In part one, Wheeler provides an historical introduction to Angola,
outlining the country's physical and social geography, the rise of Portuguese rule, and
the African reaction up to 1961. In part two, Pélissier then considers the revolt of 1961,
and its political, social and economic repercussions. Appendices include a list of
Governors-General in the colony since 1854.

62 **Angola: apontamentos sobre a colonização dos planaltos e litoral do sul de
Angola.** (Angola: remarks on the settlement of the plateaus and coast of
the south of Angola.)
Extracted from historical documents by Alfredo de Albuquerque
Felner. Lisbon: Agência Geral das Colónias, 1940. 3 vols. maps.
A documentary history of the European settlement of the Benguela plateau and coast,
consisting mainly of government reports and letters. Volume 1 deals in general with
the early colonizers, and their relations with indigenous peoples. Each of volumes 2
and 3 contains transcriptions of around sixty to seventy original documents, from the
periods 1801-55, and 1856-93 respectively.

63 **Angola: five centuries of conflict.**
Lawrence W. Henderson. Ithaca, New York: Cornell University Press,
1979. 272p.
A general history of Angola, which starts with the first Portuguese raids in 1482, and
continues until the conflicts which followed independence in 1975. The slave trade,
colonialism, and colonization are all covered in some depth, whilst a full background is

also provided on both the human and physical environment of Angola. The author lived as a missionary in colonial Angola for over twenty years.

64    **The changing historiography of Angola and Mozambique.**
Gerald J. Bender, Allen F. Isaacman.    In: *African studies since 1945: a tribute to Basil Davidson.* Edited by C. Fyfe.    London: Longman, 1976, p. 220-48.
Examines changing approaches to the study of African history after the establishment of the *Estado Novo* in Portugal in 1932, and again after the 1961 uprising in Angola.

65    **European activity and African reaction in Angola.**
Walter Rodney.    In: *Aspects of Central African history.* Edited by Terence O. Ranger.    Oxford; Portsmouth, New Hampshire: Heinemann, 1968, p. 49-70.
A brief history of the growth of both the slave trade and the more recent metropolitan capitalism in Angola, which specifically examines the reaction of Africans, which took the form of rebellions and revolts. Other chapters in the book cover neighbouring countries, placing the Angolan situation in perspective.

66    **Historical dictionary of Angola.**
Phyllis M. Martin.    Metuchen, New York: Scarecrow, 1980. 174p. bibliog.
This reference work contains an extensive list of names of geographical areas and features, ethnic groups, institutions, public figures and words in common usage, with short explanations in English. In addition, the dictionary includes a brief chronology of Angola's history, tables containing demographic and economic data mainly from the 1960s and 1970s, a short historical and geographical outline of the country, and a full bibliography.

67    **History of central Africa.**
Edited by David Birmingham, Phyllis Martin.    London: Longman, 1983. 2 vols. maps. bibliog.
A major work on the history of central Africa, from before European contact with the region to the early 1980s, including chapters by a number of prominent historians of the area. Volume 1 deals with pre-colonial societies by region: a chapter by Jan Vansina on 'The peoples of the forest' (p. 75-117) provides an introduction to village life in northern Angola and the Congo, as well as early African kingdoms, intercontinental trade, and the agricultural revolution after 1600. The following chapter, by Joseph C. Miller on 'The paradoxes of impoverishment in the Atlantic Zone' then concentrates more directly on Angola, stressing the growth of opportunities, and intensified struggle in response to slaving and 'legitimate' trade. Volume 2 deals with more recent history, in the case of Angola, up to 1961. In particular, a chapter by W. G. Clarence-Smith on 'Capital accumulation and class formation in Angola' (p. 163-99) emphasizes the similarities between the pattern of Portuguese colonialism and that of other European powers.

68  **In the eye of the storm: Angola's people.**
    Basil Davidson.   London: Longman; Harmondsworth, England:
    Penguin, 1972. 355p. bibliog.

A passionate historical account of Angola's struggle against Portuguese rule written before independence. The book is divided into three main sections, covering the period prior to and during the slave trade; the late 19th and early 20th centuries during which the Portuguese expanded their sphere of influence, and finally the guerilla war from the 1960s onwards. It focuses on the Angolan people's own response to external aggression, and vigorously challenges the colonial argument that African's were incapable of self-government. A brief final section considers the necessity for a revolutionary transformation of Angolan society. The author travelled widely in Angola as a guest of the MPLA, and the book includes numerous individual testimonies on colonialism and the armed struggle.

69  **Luanda, Angola: the development of internal forms and functional patterns.**
    Ladd Lind Johnson.   PhD thesis, University of California, Los Angeles,
    California, 1970. (Available from University Microfilms, Ann Arbor,
    Michigan, order no. 70-19858).

A historical geography of Luanda, from its first period of growth in the 16th and 17th centuries, through to the modern development of both downtown and shanty areas. There is an extensive discussion of the urban morphology of the late colonial period, including the issues of residential and industrial zoning, and current planning problems.

70  **Portugal in Africa.**
    James Duffy.   Harmondsworth, England: Penguin, 1962. 240p. maps.
    bibliog.

A short and accessible history of Portuguese colonial rule in Africa up to 1961, based on the author's earlier volume *Portuguese Africa* (Cambridge, Massuchussets: Harvard University Press, 1959), which focuses mainly on Angola and Mozambique. Divided into three parts, the first outlines early Portuguese explorations, with one chapter devoted exclusively to Angola between the 16th and 19th centuries. Part 2 then deals with both the international political disputes over Africa in the late 19th century, and the construction of an economic system based on forced labour. Finally, part 3 reflects on political and economic realities in the Portuguese colonies in the 1960s, compared to the rhetoric of the colonial government. It also charts the growth of African and world opposition to Portuguese policies.

71  **Protest and resistance in Angola and Brazil: comparative studies.**
    Edited by Ronald H. Chilcote.   Berkeley, California: University of
    California Press, 1972. 317p. bibliog.

This edited volume includes four chapters on Angola, and three that provide a comparative overview of Angola and Brazil. In the first part of the book, a chapter by David Birmingham analyses initial responses of the African population to the Portuguese. This is followed by an examination of the Tokoist church, by Alfredo Margarido. The Church was an ambiguous movement, but one which achieved considerable strength. It preached passivity to the colonial state, but fostered an acute awareness of exploitation. In a third chapter, Michael Samuels considers early attempts to bring educational reforms to the colony, led by Antonio Joaquim de Miranda, whilst the subsequent chapter by Douglas Wheeler concerns Angolan resistance as manifested in the protest writings of *assmilados* at the turn of the century. Later, two comparative chapters by Marvin Harris and Roger Bastide focus on the role of the Portuguese state, and Portuguese Catholicism respectively, and their impact on the two countries. Finally, Ronald Chilcote synthesizes and classifies the protest movements of the two countries.

**Angola: five centuries of Portuguese exploitation.**
*See* item no. 247.

# African societies

72 **The African middle ages, 1400-1800.**
Roland Oliver, Anthony Atmore.   Cambridge, England: Cambridge University Press, 1981. 216p. maps. bibliog.
An essential introduction to African history in the period 1400-1800, published to coincide with the third edition of the authors' earlier volume *Africa since 1800* (q.v.). Chapter 11, 'The land of the blacksmith kings', focuses directly on the Kongo kingdom of what is now Angola. Other chapters deal with surrounding areas. Like its sister volume, the book includes a number of very useful maps showing the approximate areal extent of African states, as well as patterns of pre-colonial migration and influence.

73 **L'ancien Congo d'après les archives romaines (1518-1640).** (The ancient Kongo according to Roman archives [1518-1640].)
(Mgr.) Jean Cuvelier, (Abbot) Louis Jadin.   Brussels: Académie Royale de Science Coloniale, 1954. 600p. maps. (Memoires de l'Académie, no. 36).
After a discussion of the role of missionaries in the Kongo kingdom in the 16th and early 17th centuries, this book presents over 200 contemporary documents relating to the Kongo kingdom, and missionary activity there, each translated into French, with annotations.

74 **L'ancien Congo et l'Angola, 1639-1655, d'après les archives romaines, portugais, néerlandaises et espagnols.** (The ancient Congo and Angola, 1639-1655, based on the Roman, Portuguese, Dutch and Spanish archives.)
Edited by Louis Jadin.   Brussels: Institute Historique Belge de Rome, 1975. 3 vols. (Bulletin, Institute Historique Belge de Rome, vols. 39-41).
A total of 859 original documents from 17th century Angola, translated into French and annotated by the editor. Of these, 190 are from the archives of the Dutch West India Company; over 300 letters are from the archives of the Capuchin archives in Rome; around 200 letters and reports are from the *Arquivo Histórico Ultramarino*, and

the *Torre do Tombo* in Lisbon; there are 30 diplomatic letters from João IV of Portugal to his agents in Paris and Rome from the archives and libraries of Évora in Portugal; whilst the remainder are documents relating to four missions by Italian and Spanish Capuchin friars to Angola between 1619-54, from Spanish archives.

75    **L'ancien royaume du Congo des origines à la fin du XIXe siécle.** (The
      ancient Kongo kingdom from its origins to the end of the 16th century.)
      W. G. L. Randles.    Paris: Mouton, 1968. 275p. maps. bibliog.
      (Civilizations et Societés, no. 14).

A history of the Kongo kingdom prior to the arrival of the Portuguese, and through the early stages of contact. An excellent narrative covers state institutions, the élite classes and the economy, before examining the European impact on them, including the effects of conversion to Christianity. The book stresses that existing African structures were adapted in response to the European presence rather than being replaced as a result of some 'European civilizing mission'.

76    **Beyond decline: the kingdom of the Kongo in the 18th and 19th centuries.**
      Susan Harlin Broadhead.    *International Journal of African Historical
      Studies*, vol. 12, no. 4 (1979), p. 615-50.

Analyses the decline of power of the Kongo kingdom, normally supposed to have resulted from Portuguese conquest in the 17th century. In contrast to this theory, Broadhead argues that the relatively weak rural-based monarchy established by Pedro IV in the early 18th century continued to survive, albeit with a fluid and changing status, until exposure to international commerce in the late 19th century. It was this which finally weakened the aristocracy, and with it, the monarchy.

77    **Daily life in the kingdom of the Kongo.**
      Georges Balandier, translated from the French by Helen Weaver.
      London: Allen and Unwin, 1968. 288p. bibliog. (Daily Life Series,
      no. 9).

A social history of the Kongo from the beginning of the 16th century, in the reign of Nzinga Mbemba Afonso (1506-1543), through to the near collapse of the kingdom in the 18th century. The work is based on contemporary accounts of social life and customs, and considers both royal households and ordinary people on either side of the Congo river. It includes a bibliography of relevant documents, mainly in French translation.

78    **The dark kingdoms: the impact of white civilization on three great
      African monarchies.**
      Alan Scholefield.    London: Heinemann, 1975. 194p. maps. bibliog.

A comparative history of the Kongo kingdom under Afonso I, and the kingdoms of Mosheh in Lesotho, and Glélé in Dahomey (now Benin). The section on the Kongo kingdom (p. 3-51), however, is based rather heavily on reiteration of the comments of early travellers. It argues somewhat unconvincingly that the flourishing kingdom of the Kongo 'might have been a watershed for a multi-racial Africa'. Included are several engravings of the Kongo.

79 **Descipção da história dos três reinos do Congo, Matamba e Angola.**
(Description of the history of the three kingdoms of Kongo, Matamba
and Angola.)
(Padre) Giovanni António Cavazzi de Montecuccolo, translated from
the Italian and edited by (Padre) Graciano Maria de Leguzzano.
Lisbon: Junta de Investigações do Ultramar, 1965. 2 vols. maps. bibliog.
A Portuguese translation of the work of the Capuchin missionary P. Cavazzi, first
published in Bologna in 1687 as *Istorica descrizione de tré regni Congo, Matamba et
Angola*. It is annotated, with an appendix containing sixty-eight relevant contemporary
documents, a chronological index from 1618-94, and a glossary of names of people and
places in the three kingdoms. Along with the work of Pigafetta (q.v.), this is one of the
prime sources on early Angola produced by the Capuchin missions.

80 **Early Kongo-Portuguese relations: a new interpretation.**
John K. Thornton. *History in Africa*, vol. 8 (1981), p. 183-204.
Argues that studies of the history of the Kongo kingdom of the 17th to 19th centuries
have exaggerated the significance of relations with Portugal. The author suggests that
this results from the fact that the only available historical sources are the documents
of Portuguese travellers, officials and missionaries.

81 **European sources for sub-Saharan Africa before 1900: use and abuse.**
Edited by Beatrix Heintze, Adam Jones. *Paideuma: Mitteilungen zur
Kulturkunde* (Stuttgart), vol. 33 (1989), 445p.
A special edition of the journal *Paideuma*, which is devoted to European sources on
African history. Four articles refer directly to Angola. These are: 'Written sources,
oral traditions, and oral traditions as written sources: the steep and thorny way to early
Angolan history', by Beatrix Heintze (p. 263-88), which includes various genealogies
of the kings of Ndongo, based on different European sources; 'European sources for
the study of religious changes in 16th and 17th century Kongo', by Anne Hilton
(p. 289-312); 'The chronicle as source, history and hagiography: the Católogo dos
Governadores de Angola', by John K. Thornton and Joseph C. Miller (p. 359-90),
which notes that this 18th century chronicle was written by various local authors, often
correcting each others' work; and 'The correspondence of the Kongo kings, 1614-35:
problems of internal written evidence on a central African kingdom', by John K.
Thornton (p. 407-22). Other useful general articles by Jan Vansina and John D. Fage
discuss other difficulties with European sources.

82 **The kingdom of Kongo.**
Anne Hilton. Oxford: Clarendon Press, 1985. 319p. maps. bibliog.
(Oxford Studies in African Affairs).
A general history of the rise and fall of the Kongo kingdom, from prior to European
contact, through to the early 20th century. Individual chapters deal with the
background to Kongo society; the first contacts with Europeans; the centralization, and
subsequent decentralization of the kingdom around the turn of the 17th century; the
period of Dutch occupation of Luanda; followed by the Portuguese restoration and
eventual demise of the Kongo kingdom as a major force. The work is based on
contemporary documentary evidence, and contains a full and useful list of historical
archives.

83 **The kingdom of Kongo: civil war and transition, 1641-1718.**
John K. Thornton. Madison, Wisconsin: University of Wisconsin
Press, 1983. 193p. maps. bibliog.

A reconstruction of the history and social conditions of the period based on contemporary documents. The book analyses the decline of the centralized political system of the Kongo kingdom, and the radical transformation of society, looking in detail at conditions in the villages and towns through the civil wars of the 17th century. It argues that processes internal to the kingdom hastened its decline, placing less emphasis on the role of European contact.

84 **Kingdoms of the savannah.**
Jan Vansina. Madison, Wisconsin: Wisconsin University Press, 1966. 364p. bibliog.

A first rate history of the precolonial and colonial era in the grasslands of Angola and Zambia to the south of the rain forest zone, dealing with the kingdoms of Kongo, Ndongo and Matamba; the Lunda and Luba empires; and the Chokwe nation, from 1600-1900. This book is a classic work, combining documentary evidence, mainly from Portuguese sources, with a rich trawl of oral traditions based on original anthropological field research.

85 **Kings and kinsmen: early Mbundu states in Angola.**
Joseph C. Miller. London: Clarendon, 1976. 312p. maps. bibliog.
(Oxford Studies in African Affairs).

Based on oral testimonies collected in the country during 1969-1970, this work provides a detailed history and explanation of the formation of the Ndongo, Matemba and Kassanje states of the Mbundu of northwestern Angola. It shows how the Mbundu built up complex political structures in the centuries up to the establishment of the small Portuguese state of the 17th century, and also explores the thought and behaviour of the state-builders. It argues that state-like institutions spread through the region not by conquest or simple migration, but through a long historical process of adaptation and modification. In charting this process, the book also challenges the popular notion that little had changed in Angola before the Portuguese disturbed an assumed static equlibrium of society.

86 **Kongo: le lignage contre l'Etat.** (Kongo: lineage versus the state.)
António Custódio Gonçalves. Lisbon: Instituto de Investigação
Científica Tropical; Évora, Portugal: Universidade de Évora, 1985.
255p. maps. bibliog.

A study of the development of the Kongo kingdom from the start of the 16th century to the beginning of the 18th century. The book first charts the history of migration, lineage, and alliances of the Mbanza Kongo, before analysing the evolution of traditional state structure, political economy, and ideologies through this period. An important work.

87  **Pre-colonial African trade: essays on trade in central and eastern Africa before 1900.**
Edited by Richard Gray, David Birmingham.  London: Oxford University Press, 1970. 308p. maps. bibliog.
This collection of essays includes three chapters of interest on Angola. Chapter 7, by Phyllis Martin, covers trade between the Vili Loango and the Portuguese along the coast to the north of present-day Angola (including Cabinda) in the 17th and 18th centuries. Subsequent chapters by David Birmingham and Joseph Miller focus respectively on early African trade in Angola as a whole, and on trade in the Chokwe region of eastern Angola in the 19th century. Miller argues that Chokwe expansion was based first on trade in wax and ivory, and only later on trading of slaves with the Portuguese. Birmingham too suggests that long-distance, but internal trade, for example in salt, was more important at an earlier date than previously was suggested.

88  **A report of the kingdom of Kongo and of surrounding countries, drawn out of the writings and discourses of the Portuguese, Duarte Lopes.**
Filippo Pigafetta, translated from the Italian and edited by M. Hutchinson.  London: Frank Cass, 1970. 2nd ed. 174p. maps.
A contemporary description of the Kongo kingdom based on the journey of Portuguese explorer Duarte Lopes to Angola in 1578. Divided into two books, the first contains a detailed description of each area visited, whilst the second describes the city of San Salvador, the development of Christianity there, the invasions of the Jagas, and various matters concerning the royal court and succession. There is also a map of the Kongo prepared by Pigafetta, and based again on an original by Lopes. The original Italian version, *Relatione del regno di Congo et delle circonvince contrade tratta dalli scritti e ragionamenti di Oduarte Lopez Portoghese* (Rome: B. Grassi, 1591) is also available in facsimile, edited by Rosa Capeans (Lisbon: Agência Geral das Colónias, 1942). The first English edition appeared in 1881, published by John Murray of London.

89  **The strange adventures of Andrew Battell of Leigh in Angola and the adjoining regions.**
Edited by E. G. Ravenstein.  London: Hakluyt Society, 1901. 210p. maps. bibliog.
A description of the travels of Andrew Battell in Kongo and Angola, presented by E. G. Ravenstein. Battell was one of four English seamen known to have visited Angola towards the end of the 16th century, after being captured off the Brazilian coast by the Portuguese. His copious notes describe his capture, imprisonment and escape in Angola; the subsequent invasion of the Gagas; the military activities of the Portuguese; as well as a general description of the various provinces he visited, covering peoples, customs and wildlife. This edition also includes a report of notes on the 'religion and customs of Angola, Congo and Loango', taken from *Purchase his pilgrimes* (London: H. Featherstone, 1617), based again on the account of Battell, and also of Thomas Turner. Five appendices then cover extracts of Anthony Knivet's diary of travels in the Kongo; an outline on the history of the Kongo to the end of the 17th century by Ravenstein; a list of the kings of Kongo; an outline of the history of Angola in the same period, again by Ravenstein; and a list of the governors of Angola.

90   **Trade and conflict in Angola: the Mbundu and their neighbours under the influence of the Portuguese, 1483-1790.**
David Birmingham.   Oxford: Clarendon, 1966. 178p. maps. bibliog.
(Oxford Studies in African Affairs).
An important work, examining the impact of Portuguese colonialism in Angola within the framework of African, rather than European history. The book spans the first three centuries of European contact with the area, and is based on a study of oral traditions and history, as recorded by early travellers, as well as Portuguese documentary records.

91   **Trade and dependency in central Africa: the Ovimbundu in the 19th century.**
Fola Soremekun.   In: *The roots of poverty in central and southern Africa*. Edited by Robin Palmer, Neil Parsons.   London: Heinemann, 1977, p. 82-95.
This article discusses Ovimbundu long-distance trade in the 19th century, which included slave trading. It argues that understanding of the extent of existing trading networks is essential to any subsequent study of the impact of colonization, and the creation of poverty and dependence in the late colonial era.

**Angola in the sixteenth century: um mundo que o português encontrou.**
(Angola in the 16th century: a world that the Portuguese found.)
*See* item no. 93.

**Demography and history in the kingdom of the Kongo.**
*See* item no. 170.

# European exploration and the slave trade, 1482-1850

92   **An account of the discoveries of the Portuguese in the interior of Angola and Mozambique.**
Thomas Edward Bowdich.   New York: AMS Press, 1980. 186p. maps.
A reprint of the original 1824 edition (London: J. Booth), this short monograph is based on documents and other information collected by the author in Lisbon on the activities of Portuguese explorers in Africa. The work also includes notes on the geography and languages of Angola.

93  **Angola in the sixteenth century: um mundo que o português encontrou.**
(Angola in the 16th century: a world that the Portuguese found.)
Joseph C. Miller.   In: *Empire in transition: the Portuguese world at the time of Camões.* Edited by Alfred Hower, Richard A. Preto-Rodas. Gainesville, Florida: University of Florida Press, 1985, p. 118-34.
An account in English of Angolan society prior to, and immediately after, the arrival of the Portuguese. The article challenges the notion of 'Lusotropicalism', in which civilized Europeans are portrayed as encountering an alien and passive Africa. It examines instead how at this early stage of contact, Africans and Europeans interacted on a relatively equal basis.

94  **Angolana: documentos sobre Angola. Volume 1: 1783-1883.** (Angolana: documents about Angola. Volume 1: 1783-1883.)
Annotated by Mário António Fernandes de Oliveira.   Luanda: Instituto de Investigação Científica de Angola; Lisbon: Centro de Estudos Históricos Ultramarinos, 1968. 848p. bibliog.
This is the first of two volumes containing letters, reports and other documents of social or political importance concerning the exploration and conquest of Angola. They are selected from the archives of the *Arquivo Histórico Ultramarino* in Lisbon, and deal with the period up to the Berlin Conference (1884-85). A second volume, selected and annotated by Mário de Oliveira and Carlos Alberto Mendes do Couto, and covering the period from 1883-87, was published in 1972.

95  **The art of war in Angola, 1575-1680.**
John K. Thornton.   *Comparative Studies in Society and History,* vol. 30 (1987), p. 360-78.
This article presents evidence from Portuguese and Spanish documents which suggest that despite superior firepower, European armies did not overwhelm the Angolan kingdom of Ndongo. The author argues that in practice, and contrary to popular belief, the Portuguese art of war changed during this period, adopting a number of African tactics and organizational principles.

96  **The Atlantic slave trade: a census.**
Philip D. Curtin.   Madison, Wisconsin: University of Wisconsin Press, 1969. 338p. maps. bibliog.
A comprehensive account of the slave trade through four centuries which provides details of the origins and destinations of slaves from various parts of Africa, and tries to establish accurate figures on the number of slaves transported. By 1600, Curtin estimates that Angola was providing around one third of all transatlantic slaves.

97  **Black mother: Africa and the Atlantic slave trade.**
Basil Davidson.   Harmondsworth, England: Penguin, 1980. 2nd ed. 304p. bibliog.
First published in 1961, this is a readable introduction to the slave trade and its effect on Africa as a whole. In part 1, the structure of the leading states in Africa prior to the arrival of Europeans is outlined, followed in parts 2-3 by a description of the development of the slave trade itself. Parts 4-6 then look at the impact of slaving

respectively on the area that is now Angola (p. 133-72), as well as the East Coast and the Gulf of Guinea.

98  **Congo to Cape: early Portuguese explorers.**
Eric Axelson. London: Faber & Faber, 1973. 224p. maps. bibliog.

An account of the explorations of Diogo Cão (1482-86) and Bartolomeu Dias (1487-88), including discussion of their discoveries in Angola.

99  **Fontes para a história de Angola do século XVII.** (Historical sources for Angola from the 17th century.)
Beatrix Heintze, Fernão de Sousa, Maria Adélia de Carvalho Mendes. Stuttgart: Franz Steiner, 1985-88. 2 vols. (Veröffentlichungen des Frobenius, Instituts an der Johann Wolfgang Goethe, Universität zu Frankfurt/Main, Studien zur Kulturkunder, Bd. 75).

A collection of over 300 documents on Angola dating from the 17th century. Volume 1 includes letters from the Governors of the province to the King of Portugal, reports and balances of provincial accounts, and descriptions of Luanda and its region. Volume 2 contains numerous supplementary letters sent between the province and metropolitan Portugal.

100  **História do Congo: Documentos.** (History of the Congo: Documents.)
(Visconde de) Paiva Manso. Lisbon: Academia Real das Ciências de Lisboa, 1877. 369p.

A collection of original documents dating from 1492-1722, arranged in chronological order, and with minimal editing or annotation. The documents mostly concern correspondence between the Portuguese monarch and his various representatives in Angola, as well as with missionaries and local dignatories.

101  **História geral das guerras Angolanas.** (General history of the Angolan wars.)
António de Oliveira de Cadornega. Lisbon: Agência Geral das Colónias, 1940-42. 3 vols.

First published in 1680, these volumes provide an eye witness account of the Angolan wars of that century, including the taking of Luanda by the Dutch. This represents a valuable primary source, although the modern editors describe some 'inaccuracies'. This set of volumes was edited by José Matias Delgado (vols 1-2) and Manuel Alves da Cunha (vol. 3).

102  **Portuguese adaptation to trade patterns: Guinea to Angola (1443-1640).**
Eugenia W. Herbert. *African Studies Review*, vol. 17, no. 2 (Sept. 1974), p. 411-23.

Although this short article contains few direct references to Angola, it does include an important argument that along the whole of the west and central African coast, the Portuguese were forced to adapt to pre-existing local patterns of exchange and trade before they were able to exploit the region.

103    **The Portuguese conquest of Angola.**
       David Birmingham.    London: Oxford University Press, 1965. 53p.
       maps.

Published under the auspices of the Institute of Race Relations, this short monograph presents material from the author's larger study of the history of the Mbundu (q.v.). Here, a brief history of Portuguese slave trading and conquest in West Central Africa up to the end of the 18th century is provided. Individual chapters cover the opening of the slave trade, subsequent wars, and the consolidation of Portuguese authority in certain areas. Finally, the rise of competing European interests in the area are considered.

104    **The Portuguese seaborne empire, 1415-1825.**
       Charles Ralph Boxer.    London: Carcanet, 1991. 2nd ed. 426p. maps.
       bibliog.

This wide ranging account of Portuguese expansion, first published in 1969 (London: Hutchinson), contains useful information on the slave trade in Angola, the Dutch occupation and recapture of Luanda, and the activities of Portuguese missionaries and traders in the colony. An earlier book by the author focused on the actions of one explorer, Salvador de Sá, but is now out of print (*Salvador de Sá and the struggle for Brazil and Angola, 1602-1686*. London: Athlone Press, 1952. 451p.).

105    **The Portuguese slave trade from Angola in the 18th century.**
       Herbert S. Klein.    In: *Forced migration: the impact of the export slave trade on African societies*. Edited by J. E. Inikori.    New York:
       Africana, 1982, p. 221-41.

This article, which first appeared in the *Journal of Economic History* (vol. 34, [1972], p. 894-918), examines the volume and organization of the slave trade in Angola. It argues that it differed from elsewhere in Africa, in that profits went to Portuguese, rather than African middlemen.

106    **Portuguese society in the tropics: the municipal councils of Goa, Macão, Bahia and Luanda, 1510-1800.**
       Charles Ralph Boxer.    Madison, Wisconsin: University of Wisconsin
       Press, 1965. 240p. maps. bibliog. (Paul Knapland Lectures, 1964
       Series).

The last of four lectures presented in this volume (p. 110-40) deals with the history of the municipal council of Luanda, based on the surviving records of the council, and of correspondence between Luanda and Lisbon up to the end of the 18th century. Comparisons are drawn throughout the book between town councils in different parts of the Portuguese Empire during this period. In the case of Luanda, political and commercial disputes between the province of Angola and central authorities in Lisbon are highlighted. Included in the book are a number of contemporary documents, translated into English, as well as a guide to primary reference sources in Luanda.

107 **Scientific explorations in the Portuguese overseas territories (1783-1808) and the role of Lisbon in the intellectual-scientific community of the late eighteenth century.**
William Joel Simon. Lisbon: Instituto de Investigação Científica Tropical, 1983. 193p. maps. bibliog.
Includes two general chapters on the role of Portugal in the development of scientific research in the 18th century, as well as a chapter (p. 79-104) which focuses on the activities of Joaquim José da Silva, a naturalist who worked for the colonial administration in Luanda. Appendix 4 contains a number of da Silva's reports and letters.

108 **The voyages of Diogo Cão and Bartholemeu Dias, 1482-88.**
Ernest George Ravenstein. Pretoria: State Library, 1986. 26p. maps.
(Reprinted from the *Geographical Journal*, vol. 16, no. 6 [Dec. 1900]).
A short description of the voyages of Cão and Dias, which although partly superceded by more recent accounts, such as that of Axelson (*see* item no. 98), still provides an interesting introduction, and includes some original maps.

109 **Way of death: merchant capitalism and the Angolan slave trade 1730-1830.**
Joseph C. Miller. Madison, Wisconsin: James Currey, 1988. 770p. maps. bibliog.
A major work on the Atlantic slave trade in the 18th and 19th centuries, that focuses on processes in Brazil and Portugal, as well as in Angola itself. The book examines how the mercantile economy of Portugal was evolving during the period, as well as presenting evidence of the attitudes and behaviour of Europeans and Africans involved in the slave trade. The author argues that the period was one in which commercialization spread into the interior of Angola, and radically altered the terms on which the slave trade was conducted, eventually leading to its decline.

**The strange adventures of Andrew Battell of Leigh in Angola and the adjoining regions.**
*See* item no. 89.

**Brève relation de la fondation de la mission des frères mineurs capucins du séraphique père saint François au royaume de Congo, et des particularités, coutumes et façons de vivre des habitants de ce royaume.** (Brief report of foundation of the mission of Capuchin monks of Fr. Saint François in the Kongo kindom, and of the particularities, customs, and ways of life of the inhabitants of that kingdom.)
*See* item no. 212.

**Fra. Girolamo Merolla da Sorrento, the congregtion of the Propaganda Fide, and the Atlantic slave trade.**
*See* item no. 215.

**A history of the American Board Missions in Angola, 1880-1940.**
*See* item no. 216.

**Misiones capuchinas em Africa. Vol 1: La mision del Congo** (Capuchin missions in Africa. Vol 1: The Congo mission.)
*See* item no. 217.

**Monumenta missionaria Africana: Africa occidental.** (African missionary activity: West Africa.)
*See* item no. 218.

**Alguns aspectos da administração de Angola em época de reformas (1834-1851).** (Some aspects of the administration of Angola in the reform period [1834-1851].)
*See* item no. 317.

# Late colonial period, 1850-1960

110  **Africa in ferment: the background and prospects of African nationalism.**
Thomas Masaji Okuma.   Boston, Massachussets: Beacon; Toronto:
S. J. Reginald Saunders, 1962. 137p.
Written by a missionary in Angola, this book presents a balanced review of the historical background to Portuguese repression during the late colonial period, and the outbreak of nationalist violence in 1961. Whilst arguing for independence, it notes the risks for Angola's future stability in Portuguese manipulation of ethnic rivalry. Includes a list of religious societies operating in Angola since 1482.

111  **Africa since 1800.**
Roland Oliver, Anthony Atmore.   Cambridge, England: Cambridge
University Press, 1981. 3rd ed. 372p. maps. bibliog.
The sister volume to *The African middle ages, 1400-1800* (q.v.), this book provides a readable introduction to African history during the colonial period and after independence, with rather limited, but nonetheless useful treatment of Angola and its neighbours. Several maps show the pattern of colonial advance in West Central Africa.

112  **An African awakening.**
Basil Davidson.   London: Jonathan Cape, 1955. 262p.
At a time of 'awakening' of African peoples, opposition to colonial rule, and growth of liberation movements in much of East, West and Southern Africa, this book paints a vivid and convincing portrait of similar stirrings in the French and Belgian Congo, and in Angola. The book is based on four years of travel in the region, and stands out as an early and powerful example of advocacy of the African cause, as well as a detailed description of the social and economic conditions of that time.

### 113 Angola in perspective: endeavour and achievement in Portuguese West Africa.
F. Clement C. Egerton.   London: Routledge & Paul, 1957. 272p. maps.

An early and avidly pro-Portuguese account of the European 'civilizing mission' in Angola, which argues that the nature of the 'Portuguese soul' led to a unique and beneficial impact on the region.

### 114 Angola without prejudice.
F. Clement C. Egerton.   Lisbon: Agency-General for the Overseas Territories, 1955. 30p.

A short rebuttal of the work of Basil Davidson, including the book *An African awakening* (*see* item no. 112), and a defence of Portuguese colonial policy in Angola during the 20th century.

### 115 Angola: secret government documents on counter-subversion.
Translated and edited by Caroline Reuver-Cohen, William Jerman.
Rome, New York: IDOC International, 1974. 172p.

Contains thirty-six secret documents detailing the counter-subversion activities of the Portuguese state in Angola, which were leaked in 1972 to the Angola Committee, an anti-colonial group in Amsterdam. The documents detail the methods used by the Portuguese army and various Angolan police and information services to respond to rebel activity. Separate sections deal with the organization of counter-subversion activities; the forced removal of populations to '*aldeamentos*'; the organization of civil defence militias; the development of political propaganda and a psychological campaign against the nationalist forces; and the promotion of rural settlement schemes. In the appendix, two official Vatican-Portuguese documents dating from the 1940s, the Portuguese government's Missionary Accord (1941), and the statement of the All Africa Conference of Churches (1973) are also included, again in English translation.

### 116 The myth and reality of Portuguese rule in Angola: a study of racial domination.
Gerald J. Bender.   PhD thesis, University of California, Los Angeles, California, 1975. (Available from University Microfilms, Ann Arbor, Michigan, order no. 76-5177).

This important thesis discusses the theory and practice of Portugal's 'civilizing' social mission in Angola. It considers in detail the ideology of 'Lusotropicalism', alongside the dynamics of miscegenation, and the growth of separate white settlement. The historical and contemporary reality of racial domination and underdevelopment is highlighted. The thesis focuses on the period since the formal end of slavery in the 19th century, through to the last days of Portuguese rule.

117 **Portugal and the scramble for Africa.**
Eric Axelson. Johannesburg: University of Witswatersrand Press, 1967. 318p. maps. bibliog.
This book on Portuguese colonial expansion in the late 19th century concentrates on Mozambique, but does include two chapters of relevance to Angola, on expeditions in the Congo from 1875-84, and on the Berlin Conference of 1884-85.

118 **Portugal in Africa: the last hundred years.**
Malyn Newitt. London: C. Hurst, 1981. 278p. maps. bibliog.
Presents a history of the Portuguese Empire in Africa as a whole, from the end of the 19th century to its collapse after the revolution of 1974. Includes chapters on colonial ideology, native policy, administration, contract labour, international relations and trade. The book argues that the changes that took place in Angola and elsewhere during this period resulted from the influence of international capital; the undermining of the colonial system as a whole is also viewed in this light.

119 **Portuguese Africa.**
Ronald H. Chilcote. Englewood Cliffs, New Jersey: Prentice Hall, 1967. 149p. maps. bibliog.
A somewhat dated historical account of the Portuguese colonies in Africa, although notes on Portuguese nationalism, Lusotropicalism, and African resistance are of interest.

120 **The Portuguese and the tropics.**
Gilberto Freyre. Lisbon: Executive Committee for the Commemoration of the Vth Centenary of the Death of Prince Henry the Navigator, 1961. 296p.
A definitive statement of the 'theory' of Lusotropicality - a collection of ideas based around the theme that Portugal had a special civilizing mission in the tropics. Although there is no section devoted specifically to Angola, the book is relevant as the most comprehensive English language statement of this important, though discredited, set of ideas on colonial history, which lent 'academic' support to continued Portuguese rule in Africa.

121 **Production, trade and power: the political economy of central Angola, 1850-1930.**
Linda Marinda Heywood. PhD thesis, Columbia University, New York, 1985. (Available from University Microfilms, Ann Arbor, Michigan, order no. 8427410).
This study focuses on how the Ovimbundu responded to changing commercial and political opportunities in the latter part of the 19th, and early 20th centuries. After a discussion of the economic conditions of Ovimbundu society in the mid 19th century, the work considers the growth of commerce in rubber and the decline of the slave trade; subsequent European military conquest; and the thwarting of attempts to build a peasant society based on maize production. The emphasis throughout is on Ovimbundu resistance to colonial economic manipulation, challenging the notion that proletarianization was inevitable.

122   **A question of slavery.**
      James Duffy.   Oxford: Clarendon, 1967. 240p. maps.
A history of slavery in Angola and Mozambique in the latter part of the 19th century
and the first two decades of the 20th century, based on documentary sources in the UK
and Portugal. Two chapters are devoted exclusively to Angola, whilst four more deal
with themes that applied to both colonies, including the protests aroused in England,
and the reaction of the Portuguese government.

123   **The rose-coloured map. Portugal's attempt to build an African empire
      from the Atlantic to the Indian Ocean.**
      Charles E. Nowell.   Lisbon: Junta de Investigações Científicas do
      Ultramar, 1982. 273p. maps. bibliog. (Centro de Estudos de
      Cartografia Antiga, Estudos de Cartografia Antiga, Memórias, no. 21).
A history of Portuguese expansion in Africa in the late 19th century, which focuses
specifically on the role of explorers. It examines some of the practical reasons why
Portugal tried and failed to establish a corridor of territory stretching across southern
Africa from Angola to Mozambique. Subsequent explorations within the interior of
Angola are also considered in depth. Included are several useful maps showing the
routes of various scientific and diplomatic expeditions throughout the latter part of the
century, as well as a copy of the final version of the 'rose-coloured map' published in
1887 by the Portuguese foreign office.

124   **Slaves, peasants and capitalists in southern Angola, 1840-1926.**
      William Gervase Clarence-Smith.   Cambridge, England: Cambridge
      University Press, 1979. 132p. bibliog. (African Studies Series, no. 27).
An account of the development of different class divisions in the society and economy
of southern Angola in the late 19th and early 20th centuries. After an introduction
which sets the natural, cultural, and colonial contexts of the region, the bulk of the
book is concerned with economy, society and politics in first the colonial sector of the
economy, and then the emergent peasant sector. The author argues that there was a
growing proletarianization of former slaves in the latter part of the 19th century, with
implications for subsequent struggles in the country. In addition, the dynamic role of
local colonial capitalists in influencing both local and national state policy is
considered.

**Aspectos do povoamento branco de Angola.** (Aspects of the white colonization of Angola.)
*See* item no. 168.

**Angola under the Portuguese: the myth and the reality.**
*See* item no. 245.

**The growth and decline of African agriculture in central Angola, 1890-1950.**
*See* item no. 411.

**Trabalho. Boletim do Instituto do Trabalho, Previdência e Acçao Social.**
(Employment. Bulletin of the Institute of Employment, Social Security and
Social Work.)
*See* item no. 424.

# Armed struggle

125   **The African liberation reader.**
Edited by Aquino de Bragança, Immanuel Wallerstein.   London: Zed,
1982. 3 vols.
Selected articles, speeches and other materials from African liberation movements
collected in 1974, and published in English. Volume 1 covers the anatomy of
colonialism, with documents on the Portuguese and British colonial Empires, and the
social classes, and various cultural and religious groups that existed under colonialism.
Volume 2 then charts the rise of national liberation movements, whilst volume 3
includes material that reflects the differing strategies of these movements across the
continent. Most of the documents are taken from the former Portuguese colonies,
Namibia, Zimbabwe and South Africa, and there is a fair selection from Angola.

126   **Angola after independence: struggle for supremacy.**
*Conflict Studies*, no. 64, (Nov. 1975), 15p.
An anaylsis of the strategic situation in Angola written at the time of independence by
the London-based Institute for the Study of Conflict. It concluded that the MPLA
would dominate Angolan politics, providing a base for Soviet expansion and
subversion of the remaining white-ruled states of southern Africa. Includes some useful
information on Soviet support for the MPLA.

127   **Angola and Mozambique: the case against Portugal.**
Anders Ehnmark, Per Wästberg, translated from the Swedish by Paul
Britten-Austin, 1963. 176p. maps.
This book is in two parts, each written independently of the other. The first, by
Ehnmark (p. 11-89) deals with Angola in the aftermath of the 1961 uprising. It
includes chapters on the revolt itself, and the rebel movements, based on interviews
with refugees, as well as criticizing Portugal's continued colonial role.

128   **Angola: report of the mission of the World Assembly of Youth.**
New York: World Assembly of Youth, 1962. 53p. maps.
This report provides a useful introduction to the political turmoil in Angola after the
1961 uprising. There is also a section on the situation of refugees in neighbouring
Congo, with several harrowing photographs.

129   **Angola: socialism at birth.**
Mozambique, Angola, Guiné Information Centre (MAGIC).
London: MAGIC, 1980. 34p.
A pamphlet outlining the background to Angola's independence, including the armed
struggle of the MPLA and the subsequent 'second war of liberation'; economic and
social conditions in the new state; and continuing South African aggression.

130 **Angola: the road to independence.**
Fola Soremekun. Ife-Ife, Nigeria: University of Ife Press, 1983. 252p.
bibliog.

A history of the period of decolonization, from the coup in Portugal in 1974 and through the first period of civil war. The book describes the reactions inside Angola to the coup, and the initial search for a programme for decolonization amongst nationalist groups as well as outside the country, in Portugal and other interested nations. It then charts events during the period of the transitional government through to independence, and analyses the foreign influences on this process. Appendices include the texts of the Mombasa and Alvor accords, and details of some forty-five different parties and pressure groups in Angola at independence.

131 **The Angolan revolution. Volume 1: The anatomy of an explosion (1950-1962). Volume 2: Exile politics and guerilla warfare (1962-1976).**
John Marcum. Cambridge, Massachussets: MIT Press, 1969-78. 2
vols. maps. bibliog. (Studies in Communism, Revisionism and
Revolution).

Volume 1 of this two-volume series provides a comprehensive history of the revolution from the viewpoint of the MPLA. The work is divided into three parts. The first charts the rise of nationalism from three sources, the Mbundu, the Bakongo, and the Ovimbundu and Chokwe peoples. It is argued that these three groups are associated respectively with the three independence movements, the MPLA, the UPA, and UNITA. Parts 2 and 3 then deal with the outbreak of hostilities, and the manner in which these were drawn out into a protracted armed struggle. In volume 2, written after independence, a history of the armed struggle against the Portuguese is provided. It analyses the failure of attempts to forge a common alliance between nationalist groups, which resulted in continued post-independence fighting. Both volumes contain extensive appendices, which include documents from the revolutionary period, and lists of the main nationalist movements.

132 **Another day of life.**
Ryszard Kapuściński, translated from the Polish by William R. Brand
and Katarzyna Mroczkowska-Brand. New York: Harcourt, Brace,
Jovanovich; London: Picador, 1987. 136p.

A personal account of Angola in the period from Portuguese withdrawal to the declaration of independence, written by a Polish journalist. The author travelled in the MPLA-controlled zone, and describes the chaos in Luanda, as well as on the northern and southern fronts in the Second War of National Liberation. The book is a curious mixture of detailed observation and philosophical reflection. It was first published in Warsaw in 1976, as *Jeszcze dzienzycia.*

133 **Emerging nationalism in Portuguese Africa: documents.**
Ronald H. Chilcote. Stanford, California: Hoover Institution Press,
1972. 646p. maps. (Hoover Institution Publications, no. 97).

Contains English translations of numerous documents selected from the author's comprehensive collection (available on microfilm in the Hoover Institution Library at Stanford University, California). Chapters 1-2 present documents explaining the attitude to the overseas territories of the Portuguese colonial government and its opponents. Chapter 3 includes selected writings of Holden Roberto, leader of the FNLA; chapter 4 covers other Angolan politicians and the intelligentsia. Chapter 8 includes declarations by various UN organizations on Portuguese Africa.

134   **The fabric of terror: three days in Angola.**
       Bernardo Teixeira.   Cape Town, Pretoria: Human & Rousseau, 1965. 176p.

With an introduction by Robert Ruark, afterword by James Burnham, and illustrations by Julio Gil, this is a dramatized account of the nationalist uprising in 1961, based on the events in Uíge district. It catalogues atrocities carried out by the 'terrorists' of UPA, whilst the afterword defends Portuguese rule in the colony.

135   **Fire power.**
       Chris Dempster, Dave Tomkins, with Michel Parry.   London: Corgi, 1978. 491p.

The personal story of two English mercenaries who fought on the side of the FNLA in the post-independence struggle, and witnessed the execution of colleagues for refusing to fight, on the order of their group's commander, Colonel Callan. Part 1 describes the recruitment of mercenaries worldwide, and especially from the UK; part 2 focuses on their experiences of war in Angola, written in 'best-seller' style.

136   **Liberation movements in Lusophone Africa. Serials from the collection of Immanuel Wallerstein.**
       Chicago: Center for Research Libraries, Cooperative Africana Microforms Project, 1976/77. 3 reels of microfilm.

A microfilm of a collection of serials issued by the FNLA, MPLA, UNITA, and other independence movements in Angola, Mozambique and Guinea-Bissau. The first reel includes a complete guide to the contents, which is followed by the material relevant to Angola. It was made by Yale University Library, Photographic Services.

137   **Liberation Support Movement interview MPLA sixth region commander, Seta Likambuila.**
       Richmond, British Columbia: Liberation Support Movement, 1970. 35p.

This pamphlet reproduces the text of an interview with Seta Likambuila conducted by Don Barnett of the Canada-based Liberation Support Movement. It is of interest for its first hand information on conditions in the 'liberated zones' held by the MPLA towards the end of the armed struggle against colonialism.

138   **Modern African wars (2): Angola and Moçambique, 1961-74.**
       Peter Abbott, Manuel Ribeiro Rodrigues.   London: Osprey, 1988. 48p. maps. (Men-at-Arms Series).

A pamphlet which discusses aspects of the Portuguese defeat in Angola, Mozambique, and Guinea-Bissau. It includes colour plates of soldiers' and guerillas' uniforms, and descriptions of the arms carried by each side in the liberation war.

139 **Operation Timber: papers from the Savimbi dossier.**
Edited with an introduction by William Minter, 1988. 117p. maps.
bibliog.

Provides an introduction to the revolutionary struggle in Angola, and tensions in the
nationalist camp, before presenting English translations of documents that implicate
Jonas Savimbi, the UNITA leader, as a military collaborator with the Portuguese
against the MPLA before independence. The authenticity of the documents, and the
reality of the alliance, codenamed 'Operation Timber', are challenged by UNITA.

140 **The people's cause: a history of guerillas in Africa.**
Basil Davidson.   London: Longman, 1981. 210p. bibliog.

An Africa-wide survey of 'people's war', in which discussion of the Angolan struggle
for independence plays an important part. In particular, chapter 11 focuses on armed
struggle in Angola and the other Portuguese colonies, whilst the final two chapters go
on to place these and other struggles within a typology of guerila or irregular warfare.
The book includes some discussion of tactics and weaponry, as well as outlining a
'political economy of armed struggle'. Also included is a short guide to sources.

141 **People's war in Angola, Mozambique, and Guinea-Bissau.**
Thomas H. Henriksen.   *Journal of Modern African Studies*, vol. 14,
no. 3 (1976), p. 377-99.

This article stresses the diverse origins and development of African nationalist
movements through a comparative analysis of the typical zones of warfare,
preparations for insurgency, terrain and sanctuaries, insurgent-held zones, international aid, politicization, factionalism, and level of warfare in these three former
Portuguese colonies. Henriksen concludes that the MPLA, along with the PAIGC of
Guinea-Bissau, had its roots in European communism, but represented an
adaptation, and not a satellite of this ideology.

142 **Portugal and the press, 1961-1972.**
Lisbon: Panorama Books, 1973. 586p.

This collection of European press reports about Portugal contains many articles
focusing on the war in Angola. They are reproduced in their original language, and in
chronological order, without further comment.

143 **Portugal's African wars: Angola, Guinea-Bissau, Mozambique.**
Arslan Humbaraci, Nicole Muchnik.   New York: Third Press;
Dar-es-Salaam: Tanzania Publishing House, 1974. 250p. maps. bibliog.

Written just after the 1974 Revolution in Portugal, but before it became clear that the
new régime would grant independence to its African colonies, this book outlines the
history of the armed struggle, concentrating on Portuguese policy, but also including
individual chapters which focus on Angola.

144 **The revolution in Angola: MPLA, life histories and documents.**
Edited by Don Barnett, Roy Harvey.   Indianapolis, Indiana:
Bobbs-Merrill, 1972. 312p.

A collection of fourteen articles, interviews, communiqués and personal testimonies, which include two broadcast speeches of Agostinho Neto, a submission of the MPLA to the United Nations Committee on Decolonization, three interviews with MPLA commanders, and several detailed life histories and personal accounts of the armed struggle recorded from ordinary members of the MPLA. Also included are articles on the armed struggle which had appeared in western newspapers, notably *The Guardian*. The book also contains a number of photographs depicting life in the areas of Angola controlled by the MPLA, along with portraits of dignitaries and pictures of political meetings of the Movement.

145 **Southern Africa stands up: the revolutions in Angola, Mozambique, Zimbabwe, Namibia and South Africa.**
Wilfried Burchett.   New York: Urizen Books, 1978. 321p. maps.
bibliog.

An account of the revolutions in southern Africa during the 1970s, of which about one third deals directly with Angola. The book is based on personal interviews with senior figures in the revolution, including leading members of the MPLA and UNITA, as well as with Portuguese and Cuban actors in the liberation struggle.

146 **The struggle for Africa.**
Edited by Mai Palmberg, translated from the Swedish by E. M. K.
Andrée, Mai Palmberg, Howard Simson.   London: Zed, 1983. 286p.
maps. bibliog.

Originally published in 1982, this book aimed to provide material for discussion groups in schools and organizations on the subject of the liberation struggles. The chapter on Angola (p. 140-75) includes information on the background to Portuguese colonialism, as well as considering the armed struggle before and after independence. It is sprinkled with keywords, photographs and cartoons. There are suggested topics for discussion and lists for further reading are supplied.

147 **The terror fighters: a profile of guerilla warfare.**
Al J. Ventnor.   Cape Town: Purnell, 1969. 152p.

A personal portrait of the middle stages of the war between the Portuguese and nationalist groups in the late 1960s, based on an eyewitness account alongside the Portuguese armed forces. The book is sympathetic to the Portuguese, and warns of the dangers for South Africa in the event of a rebel victory. It is illustrated with many photographs by Cloete Breytenbach, of war operations, as well as of life in the Portuguese-held areas.

148 **The war in Angola: a socio-economic study.**
Mário de Andrade, Marc Ollivier, translated from the French by Marga
Holness.   Dar-es-Salaam: Tanzania Publishing House, 1975. 128p.
bibliog.

A concise and readable explanation of the causes of the revolution, written by the
former President of the MPLA, and a French co-writer. This is required reading for
anyone concerned with the origins of, and justification for, the liberation struggle in
Angola. Starting with the geography and history of the colony up to 1961, and the
organization of the colonial economic system, based on forced labour and exploitation,
the book goes on to consider the effects of the liberation war on this system, and socio-
economic and political changes after 1961. A short third section considers Angola as
part of a wider imperialist strategy. First published in French, as *La guerre en Angola*
(Paris: François Mespero, 1971).

149 **With freedom in their eyes.**
Laurie Gitlin (et al.).   San Francisco: People's Press, 1976. 80p.
bibliog. (People's Press Angola Book Project).

A book consisting mainly of photographs by Robert Kramer, celebrating the Angolan
revolution. The accompanying text urges support for the MPLA, and criticizes foreign
interventions and colonial rule.

**Angola: repression and revolt in Portuguese Africa.**
*See* item no. 248.

**Agostinho Neto.**
*See* item no. 283.

# Anthropology and Ethnography

150 **Angola: bibliografia antropológica.** (Angola: anthropological
bibliography.)
M. L. Rodrigues de Areia.   Coimbra, Portugal: Centro de Estudos
Africanos, Instituto de Antropologia, Universidade de Coimbra, 1984.
165p.

Arranged alphabetically by author and serial title, this bibliography provides a simple
reference of over 1600 works on Angolan anthropology and ethnography, mainly in
Portuguese, but also in English and French.

151 **Angola: os símbolos do poder na sociedade tradicional.** (Angola: the
symbols of power in traditional society.)
Edited by Manuel Laranjeira, M. L. Rodrigues de Areia.   Coimbra,
Portugal: Instituto de Antropologia, Universidade de Coimbra, 1983.
98p. bibliogs. (Publicaçoes do Centro de Estudos Africanos, no. 1).

An important volume, containing five articles, each dealing with the symbols of
political power of diverse ethnic groups in Angola. Two are in Portuguese, and
examine the Cabinda enclave (p. 11-26) and the general question of the relationship
between symbols and real political power (p. 49-66). The remaining three are in
French, and are concerned with power structures in the Kongo (p. 27-48), the royal
household of the Ovimbundu (p. 67-80), and the importance of the study of power in
anthropology (p. 81-98). Many photographs are included of the symbols described by
the text.

Anthropology and Ethnography

## 152 Bushmen and other non-Bantu peoples of Angola.
António de Almeida. Johannesburg: Witswatersrand University
Press, for the Institute for the Study of Man in Africa, 1965. 43p. maps.
bibliog.

The text of three lectures by the author, then Director of the Anthropobiological
Survey of Angola, given in Johannesburg in 1959, and edited by Phillip V. Tobias and
John Blackup. The three lectures focus respectively on 'The Yellow Bushmen
(Kwankhala and Sekele)', 'The Black Bushmen (Zama or Kwengo)', and 'The Kwádi
(Kuroka or Kwépe)', all groups located in southern Angola. Includes a select
bibliography of work by the author and his daughter in Portuguese.

## 153 Bushmen of central Angola.
D. F. Bleek. *Bantu Studies* (Johannesburg), vol. 3 (1927), p. 105-25.

An early ethnographic account of the Bushmen of central Angola, with observations
on a range of 'physical and cultural characterstics', including cleanliness, hairdressing
and tattoos.

## 154 Custom and government in the lower Congo.
Wyatt MacGaffey. Berkeley, California: University of California
Press, 1970. 322p. maps. bibliog.

Although field research for this volume was based in the Lower Congo region of
present day Zaïre, its focus on the Bakongo group provides information of relevance to
those of similar ethnicity in northern Angola. Indeed, the area studied was one
affected by an influx of Angolan refugees during the anti-colonial struggle. In this
work, structures of traditional society, clan, lineage and kinship, as well as the
processes of exchange, marriage, funerals and land allocation are discussed in turn.

## 155 The ethnography of southwestern Angola.
Carlos Estermann, translated from Portuguese and edited by
G. D. Gibson. New York, London: Africana, 1976. 3 vols.

This three volume work by Father Estermann covers the non-Bantu peoples and the
Ambo ethnic group (volume 1), the Nyaneka and Nkumbi ethnic groups (volume 2)
and the Herero peoples (volume 3), all of which are located mainly in the southwestern
provinces of Moçamedes (now Namibe), Cunene and Huíla. The work is a classic of
Portuguese colonial ethnography.

## 156 The Kavango peoples.
Gordon D. Gibson, Thomas J. Larson, Cecilia R. McGurk.
Wiesbaden, Germany: Franz Steiner Verlag, 1981. 275p. maps. bibliog.

The Kavango peoples covered in this work live along the southern border of Angola,
on the Cubango river, as well as in adjacent parts of Namibia and Botswana. After a
general introduction, covering the physical environment, origins of the population,
recorded history and colonial administration in each state, five sections provide a
detailed introduction to the ethnography of the Kwangari, Mbundza, Sambyu, Gciriku,
and Mbukushu peoples. Each of these sections provides information on history,
economy, the life of individuals (including rituals for childbirth, death and burial),
politics and law, religion, magic, and social life. The work is based mainly on published
and unpublished documentary sources; for the Gciriku and Mbukushu, information

from primary field research is included, although in both cases, the authors worked inside Botswana rather than Angola.

157   Os kyaka de Angola: história, parentesco, organização política e
territorial. Vol 1. Abertura e história. Vol 2. O parentesco. (The Kyaka
of Angola: history, kinship, political and territorial organization. Vol 1.
Introduction and history. Vol 2. Kinship.)
Mesquitela Lima.   Lisbon: Edições Távola Redonda, Instituto de
Estudos Africanos, 1988/89. 2 vols.
The first two volumes of a major three-part study of the Kyaka ethnic group, a sub-group of the Ovimbundu. The study is based on anthropological fieldwork, archival research, as well as analysis of oral traditions, and was based in Huambo district. After an introductory background to the geology, geomorphology and ecology of Central Angola, volume 1 provides an historical sketch of the region from the 16th century to the invasion of the Jagas. Volume 2 then goes on to outline details of kinship networks, describing the 'rules' for marriage, inheritance, and relations between family members. The third volume, unavailable at the time of compilation, considers the group's political and territorial organization.

158   In pursuit of a chameleon: early ethnographic photography from Angola
in context.
Beatrix Heintze.   *History in Africa*, vol. 17 (1990), p. 131-56.
Describes the major sources of photographs by early ethnographers in Angola, and argues that they have a rich research potential, subject to overcoming a number of contextual problems.

159   In the heart of Bantuland.
Dugald Campbell.   New York: Negro Universities Press, 1969. 313p.
An ethnography of the Bakongo and other ethnic groups, based on the author's travels by foot through northern Angola, Zaïre, and Zambia. It was first published in 1922.

160   The native tribes of South West Africa.
C. H. L. Hahn, H. Vedder, L. Fourie.   London: Frank Cass, 1966.
211p.
This ethnography of Namibia includes a chapter on the Ovambu, which contains observations on Angolan members of that group.

161   The Ovimbundu of Angola.
Wilfrid D. Hambly.   Chicago, Illinois: Field Museum of Natural
History, 1934. 362p. bibliog. (Field Museum of Natural History,
Publication no. 329: Anthropological Series, vol. 21, no. 2).
A report of the Frederick H. Rawson-Field Museum Ethnological Expedition to West Africa, 1929-30, which covered much of the south and central highlands of Angola. The book provides an account of the geographical milieu of the Ovimbundu, as well as their social and cultural life; education; language; religion, and culture. This is a classic early ethnology, which is supplemented at the end by numerous photographs and sketches of individuals and artefacts.

162 **The Ovimbundu under two sovereignties: a study of social control and social change among a people of Angola.**
Adrian C. Edwards.   London: Oxford University Press, for the International African Institute, 1962. 169p. maps. bibliog.

An anthropology of the Ovimbundu based on participant observation in the Bimbe area of southern Angola, at the northern edge of the Benguela highlands. The book compares social structures in the period 1874-1911, and at the time of field research, and then goes on to discuss social control, and its maintenance through kinship and marriage networks. The area of study was chosen as the most 'conservative' of the zone inhabited by the Ovimbundu in terms of social change, defined as one in which there was very little white settlement. Nonetheless, the growing influence of colonial rule on social practices was observed.

163 **Research film study of the Himba, Zimba and Kuvale people of Angola.**
Gordon Gibson.   Washington, DC: Department of Anthropology, Smithsonian Institute, 1961-73. film.

Consisting of 5,870 ft of original film, and 10,840 ft of research print, this film on the Himba, Zimba and Kuvale ethnic groups, collected by anthropologist Gordon Gibson, is housed in the National Anthropological Film Center, 3210 l'Enfant Plaza, Washington, DC 20560.

164 **Umbundu kinship and character.**
Gladwyn M. Childs.   London: Oxford University Press, for the International African Institute, 1949. 245p. maps. bibliog.

A description of the social structure, individual development and history of the Ovimbundu, based on field research over five years during the 1930s. After an introduction to the physical 'habitat' of the Ovimbundu, the study describes political and social life, and kinship structures. Part 2 covers the development of individuals through the life cycle, and includes three chapters on educational issues. Part 3 then discusses the tribal origin and historical development of the group. It includes a synchronized chart of the events of Portuguese occupation alongside the traditional history and royal succession of the Ovimbundu.

165 **Vakwandu: history, kinship, and systems of production of an Herero people of south-west Angola.**
Carlos Laranjo Medeiros.   Lisbon: Junta de Investigações Científicas do Ultramar, 1981. 75p. bibliog.

Based on the author's anthropological fieldwork amongst the small Kwandu and Munda groups on the fringe of the Namib desert in 1970/71, this paper includes a history of the area; a detailed description of the kinship system of the Kwandu; and discussion of the connections between these and the system of production.

166 **West Central Africa Part 1: the southern Lunda and related peoples (northern Rhodesia, Belgian Congo, Angola).**
Merran McCulloch.  London: International African Institute, 1951.
110p. bibliog. (Ethnographic Survey of Africa; series editor: Daryll Forde).

The total population of Lunda and related peoples was estimated at 63,000 in the 1950s, of whom 10,000 were in Angola. This monograph, which synthesizes existing anthropological studies, deals separately with the southern Lunda and Ndembu; the Chokwe and Minungu; and the Baluena, Luchazi, Luimbe, and Mbunda. It covers their demography, 'physical and mental characteristics', language, traditions, economy and social organization.

167 **West Central Africa Part 2: the Ovimbundu of Angola.**
Merran McCulloch.  London: International African Institute, 1952.
50p. bibliog. (Ethnographic Survey of Africa; series editor: Daryll Forde).

The Ovimbundu are the main ethnic group of Angola, and were estimated to make up one third of the population in the 1950s. This study, which sets out to synthesize existing anthropological articles, covers their demography, language, traditions, economy, social organization, religion, magic and aspects of the life cycle.

# Population

## General and censuses

168 **Aspectos do povoamento branco de Angola.** (Aspects of the white colonization of Angola.)
Ilídio do Amaral. Lisbon: Junta de Investigações do Ultramar, 1960. 83p. maps.

A study of the policy of promoting white settlement in Angola, which discusses its history, as well as the distribution of Portuguese and other Europeans based on the 1950 census. There is an English summary on p. 71-79, which includes extracts of the statistics presented. There are useful maps of areas of settlement, and a discussion of the problems faced by settlers.

169 **Censo geral da população, 1940.** (General population census, 1940.)
Luanda: Imprensa Nacional, 1941-47. 12 vols.

This is the first relatively accurate modern census of Angola, conducted in 1940, and published over the course of the subsequent decade. Further censuses were published in 1950 (*Il Recenseamento geral da população. 1950.* [2nd general population census, 1950.] Luanda: Imprensa Nacional, 1953-56. 5 vols.), and in 1960 (*Il Recenseamento geral da população. 1960.* [3rd general population census, 1960.] Luanda: Imprensa Nacional, 1964. 5 vols.). A further census was carried out in 1970 (*Censo da população de 1970.* [1970 Population census] Luanda: Direcção Provincial dos Serviços da Estatística), but is unavailable in UK copyright libraries.

170 **Demography and history in the kingdom of the Kongo.**
John K. Thornton. *Journal of African History*, vol. 18, no. 4 (1977), p. 507-30.

This article challenges the assumption that there was dramatic population loss in the Kongo kingdom during or after the 17th century. A revised methodology for approaching missionary statistics is outlined, followed by detailed discussion of demographic evidence in three separate regions of the kingdom: Sonyo in the north, the centre and the east, and briefly the Mbamba in the southwest. From this evidence, Thornton estimates the population of the Kongo at just over 500,000 in 1700, rather than 2 million as in previous estimates, and concludes that the area showed steady growth to the first 20th century population census figure of 1.4 million, rather than a decline.

171   **The demography of the Portuguese territories: Angola, Mozambique and Portuguese Guinea.**
Don F. Heisel.   In: *The demography of tropical Africa*. Edited by William Brass, Ansley J. Coale, Paul Demeny, Don F. Heisel, Frank Lorimer, Anatole Romaniuk, Etienne van de Walle.   Princeton, New Jersey: Princeton University Press, 1968, p. 440-65.
A now dated account, which provides an analysis of data from the 1940 and 1950 population censuses.

172   **La population noire de l'Angola.** (The black population of Angola.)
Carlos A. da Costa Carvalho.   Lisbon: Instituto Nacional de Estatística, Centro de Estudos Demográficos (CED), 1979. 142p. bibliog. (CED, Caderno no. 6).
A demographic analysis of the black population of Angola, covering population trends, age and sex structures, rates of fertility, mortality, and marriage, and perspectives on the future development of population structures. It also includes data selected from censuses from 1940-70. The work was presented as a Masters thesis at the Catholic University of Louvain, Belgium, in 1978.

173   **Recenseamento geral da população indígena da colónia em 31 de dezembro de 1929.** (General census of the indigenous population of the colony on 31 December 1929.)
*Boletim da Agência das Colonias*, vol. 7, no. 10 (Oct. 1931).
This census is regarded as relatively inaccurate, but provides some indication of the indigenous population of Angola around the start of the *Estado Novo* in Portugal.

# Population displacement

174   **Angola Report.**
Baptist Missionary Society: Publisher unknown, 1962-67.
A weekly typed newsletter describing the work of editor and missionary David Grenfell amongst Angolan refugees in the Congo Republic. These newsletters, along with Grenfell's notes, and some annual reports, are held on microfilm in the archives of the Hoover Institution on War, Revolution and Peace at Stanford University.

175    **Displaced and drought-affected persons in the Peoples' Republic of Angola: an assessment of relief operations in the southern provinces first emergency phase.**
United Nations Disaster Relief Organization (UNDRO).    Geneva: Office of the UN Disaster Relief Coordinator, 1983. 72p.

This report reviews the situation of over 660,000 drought-affected and displaced persons in seven southern provinces in the early 1980s, and describes the United Nations relief effort from 1981-83.

176    **Human rights violations in SWAPO camps in Angola and Zambia.**
International Soceity for Human Rights (ISHR), British Section.
London: ISHR, 1989. 54p.

As well as producing hundreds of thousands of refugees and displaced people of its own, Angola has also played host to a large number of refugees from neighbouring Namibia, where the independence struggle continued until 1988. This report deals with the situation of alleged political prisoners held in SWAPO detention camps inside Angola, and in Zambia. It includes eyewitness accounts of the camps, and a list of 181 persons missing or dead, who were alleged to have fallen victims to SWAPO whilst in exile in the two countries.

177    **The integration of Angolan refugees in western and northwestern Zambia.**
Ken B. Wilson.    Oxford: Refugee Studies Programme, 1986. 124p.

Reviews the historical and current experience of Angolan refugees in Zambia. Copies are available from the Documentation Centre, Refugee Studies Programme, Queen Elizabeth House, 21 St Giles, Oxford. The Centre also contains other unpublished articles on Angolan refugees.

178    **Once the running stops: the social and economic incorporation of Angolan refugees into Zambian border villages.**
Art Hansen.    PhD thesis, Cornell University, Ithaca, New York, 1976.
(Available from University Microfilms, Ann Arbor Michigan, order no. 7801625).

A study of 'self-settled' Angolan refugees in northwestern Zambia, based on anthropological field research in the region. When refugees fled Angola in 1966, the Zambian government established camps to provide food and other assistance. However, this thesis charts the often successful strategies of refugees who were not placed in such camps, but who instead integrated with members of the same ethnic group in the border area. The refugee movement itself is seen by Hansen as the latest in a series of historical migrations of Luvale-speaking peoples in the region. Summaries can be found in two articles in the journal *Disasters*, vol. 3, no. 2 (1979), covering the assimilation of the refugees (p. 369-74), and the response of the Zambian government (p. 375-80).

179 **Refugee settlement versus settlement on government schemes: the long-term consequences for security, integration and economic development of Angolan refugees (1966-1989) in Zambia.**
Art Hansen. Geneva: United Nations Research Institute for Social Development (UNRISD), 1990. 44p.
A summary of the authors' follow-up research in 1989 to his earlier study of the self-settlement of Angolan refugees in northwestern Zambia (see item no. 178). It documents the continuing survival strategies of these refugees in the region.

180 **Report on the work of the commission sent out by the Jewish Territorial Organization under the auspices of the Portuguese government to examine the territory proposed for the purpose of a Jewish settlement in Angola.**
John Walter Gregory. London: ITO, 1913. 50p. maps.
In the context of more recent displacements of population within Angola, it is interesting to note that at the start of this century, the region was seen as a potential area for resettlement of Jewish refugees from Europe. This is the report of an expedition in which the author assessed the suitability of the Benguela plateau as an area for such resettlement. The main report describes the geology, soils, climate, agriculture, trade and political and historical background to the area, concluding that successful European settlement, free from government interference, could be established. Also included is a report of the public health of the area, by C. J. Martin; remarks on soils by Professor R. A. Berry; and in three appendices, the remarks of Sir Harry Johnston and H. W. Nevinson recommending caution; translations of articles by Colonel Freire d'Andrade, Director General of the Portuguese Colonies, and Captain João Ferreira, also suggesting a cautious, but optimistic approach to settlement; and finally the text of a placed before the Portuguese parliament authorizing Jewish settlement, along with a letter of reply from the ITO, making a number of criticisms of the bill and the concept of Jewish settlement in the area.

181 **Uprooted Angolans: from crisis to catastrophe.**
T. O. Brennan. Washington, DC: American Council for Nationalities Service, 1987. 32p. map. bibliog. (United States Committee for Refugees, Issue Paper).
Describes the events leading up to the flight of nearly 400,000 Angolans to neighbouring countries, including the Liberation War and post-independence conflicts, as well as brief information on ethnic diversity. After a further section on the socio-economic situation of the refugees, this pamphlet reflects on the prospects for peace. It estimates that 40 per cent of Angola's population have fled from their homes to seek security in camps and urban areas, representing a major headache for planners once lasting peace is achieved.

**The long road home: Angola's post-war inheritance.**
*See* item no. 228.

**Status report on the emergency situation in Africa as of 15 July 1987.**
*See* item no. 236.

# Language

## General

182 **Language and literature in Portuguese-writing Africa.**
Russell G. Hamilton. *Portuguese Studies*, vol. 2 (1986), p. 196-207.
A commentary on the debate over whether Portuguese or major African languages
should have national status in the former Portuguese colonies. It concentrates on the
Angolan case, where the debate is most advanced.

## Umbundu

183 **Dicionário Etimológico Bundo-Português.** (Etymological Umbundu-
Portuguese dictionary.)
P. Albino Alves. Lisbon: Silvas, 1951. 2 vols.
A comprehensive dictionary from Umbundu (spoken in central and southern Angola
by the Ovimbundu peoples) into English, which also includes around 2,000 indigenous
proverbs.

184 **First lessons in Umbundu.**
Helen Hurlburt Stover. [n.p.] 1918. 106p.
A basic grammar divided into 44 lessons. A copy of this unpublished text can be found
in the library of the School of Oriental and African Studies, University of London.

185  **Gramática Umbundu, a língua do centro de Angola.** (Umbundu grammar, the language of central Angola.)
(Padre) José Francisco Valente.  Lisbon: Junta de Investigações do Ultramar, 1964. 430p.
Covers phonetics, morphology, and syntax of the Umbundu language. The author also compiled, with Grégoire de Guennec, a comprehensive dictionary, *Dicionário Português-Umbundu* (Luanda: Instituto de Investigação Científica de Angola, 1972. 690p.).

186  **Introduction to the history of Umbundu: L. Magyar's records (1859) and the later sources.**
István Fodor.  Hamburg, Germany: Helmut Buske, 1983. 327p. bibliog.
A history of the Umbundu language, based on the notes and linguistic records of the Hungarian explorer László Magyar. The bulk of the text is devoted to a reconstruction of the grammatical system of Umbundu as it was in the middle of the 19th century.

187  **Observations upon the grammatical structure and use of the Umbundu, or the language of the inhabitants of Bailundu and Bihe.**
Wesley M. Stover.  Boston: Todd, 1885. 83p.
Covers the orthography, etymology and syntax of Umbundu.

188  **A sketch of Umbundu.**
Thilo C. Schadeberg.  Cologne: Rüdiger Köppe, 1990. 61p. bibliog.
(Grammatische Analysen Afrikanischer Sprachen, Band 1).
Based on linguistic work undertaken at Bié in 1981/82, this pamphlet provides a simple introduction to the Umbundu language.

189  **Vocabulary of the Umbundu language comprising Umbundu-English and English-Umbundu.**
W. H. Sanders, W. E. Gray.  Boston, Massachussetts: Beacon, 1885. 76p.
A basic vocabulary, designed for use by missionaries to southern Angola.

# Kimbundu

190  **A demographic survey of the Kimbundu-Kongo language border in Angola.**
Guy Atkins. *Boletim da Sociedade de Geografia de Lisboa*, vol. 73, nos. 7-9 (July-Sept. 1955), p. 325-47.

An enumeration of the population, language, and dialects of districts along the border between the Kimbundu and Kikongo language areas in northern Angola, based on fieldwork carried out in 1953.

191  **Kimbundu grammar/Grammática elementar do Kimbundu ou língua de Angola.** (Elementary grammar of Kimbundu, or the language of Angola.)
Héli Chatelain.  Geneva: Charles Schuchardt, 1888/89. 172p.

An elementary grammar of Kimbundu, interpreted in Portuguese, but with the meaning of most words also given in English. It includes an index, and vocabulary also in English. Chatelain, a Swiss missionary, was responsible for the translation of the Bible into Kimbundu. Unfortunately, most grammars and dictionaries of Kimbundu, the language of the Mbisple, are in Portuguese. Among the more useful is this one, because of the inclusion of some English words and phrases; also *Gramática de Kimbundu* by José L. Quintão (Lisbon: Edições Descobrimento, 1934. 237p.), which includes exercises and some vocabulary. A good dictionary is *Dicionário Kimbundu-Português*, by A. de Assis Junior (Luanda: Arguente Santos, [n.d.] 384p.), for translation from Kimbundu, and *Dicionário Portuguez-Kimbundo* by J. Pereira do Nascimento (Huíla, Angola: Typographia da Missão, 1903. 136p) for translation into Kimbundu. A much larger work, *Dicionário Complementar Português-Kimbundu-Kikongo* by P. António da Silva Maia (Cucajães, Angola: Author's edition, [n.d.] 658p.) bridges the gap also to Kikongo; a copy of this is held by the library of the School of Oriental and African Studies of the University of London.

192  **O Kimbundo prático, ou guia de conversação em Português-Kimbundo.** (Practical Kimbundu, or guide to conversation in Portuguese-Kimbundu.)
(Padre) Domingos Vieira Baião. Published by author, 1940. 83p.

A useful guide to practical Kimbundu developed for colonial officials, with phrases and conversations relating to people, families, nature and society.

193  **Mbundu-English-Portuguese dictionary with grammar and syntax.**
Amandus Johnson.  Philadephia: International Printing, 1930.
[n.p.].

A lexicon of Kimbundu, with some grammar. This work is available at the library of the School of Oriental and African Studies, in London.

# Kikongo

194 **Dictionary and grammar of the Kongo language as spoken at San Salvador.**
W. Holman Bentley. London: London Missionary Society, 1887-95.
2 vols.

A major source for the Kongo language (Kikongo) as spoken inside the territory of Angola. Also of relevance are many works on Kikongo based on dialects spoken in the neighbouring Congo Republic or in Zaïre or Cameroon, such as *Grammar of the Kongo language (Kikongo)*, by K. E. Laman, (New York: Christian Alliance Publishing Company, [n.d.] 296p.), or *A grammar of the Kongo language, as spoken in the central lower part of the lower Kongo valley*, compiled by Nils Westland (Ngangila, Kongo Free State, 1894. 236p.). Works in Portuguese include the *Dicionário prático Português-Kikongo* of the Evangelical Mission of the British Missionary Society (San Salvador do Congo, Angola, 158p, 2nd ed.), and *Gramática da língua do Congo (Dialecto Kikongo)* by José Lourenço Tavares (Luanda: Imprensa Nacional, 1915. 158p.).

195 **Grammar of the Kongo language as spoken two hundred years ago.**
Hyacinth Brusciotto de Vetralla, translated from Italian by H. Grattan Guinness. London: Hodder & Stoughton, 1882. 112p.

First printed in Rome in 1659, this basic grammar of the Kongo language was written by the Capuchin missionary, Brusciotto. Although the language itself changed somewhat in the interim, it was reprinted in the late 19th century to assist missionaries working in both the Congo and northern Angola, and needing to speak Kikongo. The translator also published a separate grammar in the same year, entitled *Grammar of the Congo language, as spoken in the cataract region below Stanley Pool* (Hodder & Stoughton, 1882. 267p.).

196 **Syntax and tone in Kongo.**
Hazel Carter. London: School of Oriental and African Studies, 1973.
340p. bibliog.

A description of the syntax and tonal pattern of Zombo, a dialect of Kikongo spoken in northern Angola.

# Other languages

197 **A brief grammar of the Chokwe language: first part.**
Thomas Couttit. Chicago, Illinois, 1916. 47p.

Contains twelve introductory lessons in Chokwe, one of the main languages of eastern Angola. No publication details are given, but a copy is available at the library of the School of Oriental and African Studies, University of London.

198 **Chokwe-English, English-Chokwe dictionary and grammar lessons.**
Malcolm Brooks MacJannet.   Vila Luso, Angola: Missão da Biula,
1949. 234p.
First published in 1927, the middle part of the work contains 30 grammar lessons.

199 **Dicionário Cokwe-Português.** (Chokwe-Portuguese dictionary.)
Adriano Barbosa.   Coimbra, Portugal: Instituto de Antropologia,
1989. 750p.
A large and comprehensive dictionary of the Chokwe language from Chokwe to
Portuguese.

200 **Elementos de gramática de Utchokwe.** (Elements of Chokwe grammar.)
João Vicente Martins.   Lisbon: Instituto de Investigação Científica
Tropical, 1990. 249p. bibliog.
Includes a description of phonetics and syntax, plus a short vocabulary from Chokwe
to Portuguese and vice versa. This is one of the more important grammars of the
Chokwe language in Portuguese.

201 **A grammar of Luvale.**
A. E. Horton.   Johannesburg: Witswatersrand University Press, 1949.
221p. (Bantu Grammatical Archives, no. 2).
A basic grammar of the Luvale language spoken across the borders of Angola, Zaïre
and Zambia. A useful dictionary was produced by the same author (*A dictionary of
Luvale*, 1953. 434p.), although this remained unpublished. Both books are available at
the library of the School of Oriental and African Studies in London.

202 **A Lunda-English vocabulary.**
C. M. N. White.   Balovale, North Rhodesia: Author's Edition, 1943.
48p.
A limited vocabulary of the Lunda language of northeast Angola, western Zambia and
southern Zaïre, based on the author's five years as a District Officer in the former
colony of Northern Rhodesia. The book was later printed by the London University
Press, in 1957. A further basic work on the Lunda language is provided by another
unpublished volume, the *English-Lunda (Ndembu) abridged dictionary with Lunda-
English basic vocabulary*, by M. K. Fisher, for which research was carried out in the
Katanga province of present day Zaïre. Both volumes can be consulted at the library of
the School of Oriental and African Studies in London.

203 **A Luvale-English phrasebook.**
C. M. N. White.   London: Heinemann, 1955. 39p.
Contains useful (and some memorable) phrases concerning village life, buying and
selling, illness, agriculture, travel, and the weather.

204 **An outline of Hungu grammar.**
Guy Atkins. *Garcia de Orta*, vol. 2, no. 2 (1954), p. 145-64.
Based on observations in the Congo province of Angola in 1953, this is the only
grammar of a language spoken at that time by a group of around 60,000 people.

205 **A short Lwena grammar.**
C. M. N. White. London: Longman, Green & Co., 1949. 87p.
A basic introduction to the Luena language, providing a useful accompaniment to the
author's earlier *Lwena-English vocabulary* (Balovale, Northern Rhodesia: edition of
author, 1944. 48p.). A short description of the structure of Luena was also compiled by
W. A. Crabtree, and published in the *Journal of the Africa Society*, vol. 10 (1911),
p. 394-400.

# Religion

206 **Among the primitive Bakongo: a record of thirty years close intercourse with the Bakongo and other tribes of equatorial Africa, with a description of their habits, customs, and religious beliefs.**
John H. Weeks.   London: Seely, Service & Co., 1914. 318p. maps.
Describes customs which the author claims are representative of the whole of the lower Congo; in practice, this book was based on the author's experiences as a missionary mainly at San Salvador (now M'banza Kongo) from 1882 until the early 20th century. The book starts with a visit to the Kongo king, describing court etiquette, it then concentrates on the social and religious life of ordinary people, ranging from their birth, courtship and marriage, to warfare, magic, death and burial.

207 **Angola.**
(Padre) António Brasio.   Pittsburgh, Pennsylvania: Duquesne University Press; Louvain, Belgium: Editions E. Nauwelaerts, 1966-71. 5 vols. (Spiritana Monumenta Historica: Series Africana).
A collection of documents relating to the Order of the Holy Ghost in Angola, covering the period from 1596-1967 in five volumes. The documents are in the original Portuguese or Latin, with a short commentary on each in French by the author. The books are part of a general series on the activities of the mission worldwide.

208 **Angola awake.**
Sid Gilchrist.   Toronto: Ryerson, 1968. 123p.
Written by a senior missionary doctor of the United Church of Canada after his return from Angola, the book is aimed at a Christian audience and 'speaks out' against Portuguese colonial rule. It provides a personal viewpoint of the colony based on many years of missionary work, a brief history of the Angola, and a discussion of the role of Christian missions, as well as some of the practical as well as political problems they faced.

209 **Angola beloved.**
T. Ernest Wilson.  Neptune, New Jersey: Loizeaux Bros, 1967. 254p.
A personal account of the author's missionary experience during forty years in Angola, much of it spent in the interior provinces of Bié and Moxico.

210 **Angola, the land of the blacksmith prince.**
John T. Tucker.  London, New York, Toronto: World Dominion
Press, 1933. 180p. map. (World Dominion Survey Series, no. 4).
A general work on Angola, written from a Christian perspective. After an introduction to the human and physical background to the country, and the early 'crusaders', the book then turns to a discussion of the growth and conditions of missionary work, with the aim of informing the planning of further missions. Included is a map detailing the location of protestant missions, and four appendices presenting statistical information on missionary activity; a discussion of the availability and distribution of Bibles in Angola by the Rev. R. Kilgour; a discussion of the areas still to be touched by missionary activity in the extreme North and South of the country; and an outline of the legal status of protestant missions. Other work by the author on Angola includes *Old and new days in Angola, Africa* (Toronto: Committee on Young Peoples Missionary Education), an account of his own missionary experience.

211 **L'Angola traditionelle: une introduction aux problèmes magico-religieux.** (Traditional Angola: an introduction to magical and religious problems.)
M. L. Rodrigues de Areia.  Coimbra, Portugal: Tipografia de
Atlántida, 1974. bibliog.
A useful study of traditional religions and their magical elements, which deals respectively with the Bakongo, Mbundu and Kiyaka of the northwest; the Chokwe, Luimbi, Ngangela, Luchazi, Baluena and Mbwela in the east; and finally the Ovimbundu, Ambo and Herero of the south of Angola.

212 **Brève relation de la fondation de la mission des frères mineurs capucins du séraphique père saint François au royaume de Congo, et des particularités, coutumes et façons de vivre des habitants de ce royaume.** (Brief report of foundation of the mission of Capuchin monks of Fr. Saint François in the Kongo kindom, and of the particularities, customs, and ways of life of the inhabitants of that kingdom.)
(Brother) Jean-François de Rome, translated from the Italian and edited by François Bontinck.  Louvain, Belgium: Ed. Nauwelaert; Paris: Béatrice-Nauwelaerts, 1964. 150p. (Publication de l'Université Lovanium de Léopoldville, no. 13).
One of the most important religious sources on the Kongo kingdom in the middle of the 17th century, written by the Capuchin missionary, François de Rome, and first published in 1648. Soon after its appearance, it was translated into both French and German. The account includes various dates, and the text of two official documents, as well as providing a detailed and sympathetic account of life in the kingdom, and the activities of the Capuchins.

213 **Currie of Chissamba (Herald of the dawn).**
John T. Tucker. Toronto: United Church of Canada, 1945. 180p.

A history and appreciation of the work of protestant missionary Walter Currie, who helped build the United Church of Canada mission in southern Angola. The book narrates events from Currie's youth in Canada through his travels, to the establishment of a mission station at Chissamba in Bié district. Here, his educational and pastoral work, his contacts with Africans and with the colonial authorities, and above all his religious mission are described.

214 **Dawn in darkest Africa.**
John H. Harris. London: Frank Cass, 1968. 308p.

First published in 1912, this work provides a perceptive account of Portuguese, Belgian, German and French missionary activity in Angola.

215 **Fra. Girolamo Merolla da Sorrento, the congregation of the Propaganda Fide, and the Atlantic slave trade.**
Richard Gray. In: *La conoscenza dell'Asie e dell'Africa in Italia nei secoli XVIII e XIX* (Knowledge of Africa and Asia in the 18th and 19th centuries.), vol. 1. Naples, 1984. [n.p].

A description of the activities of Fra. Girolamo, author of *Breve e succinta relatione del viaggio nel regno del Congo nell'Africa meridionale* (Brief and succinct report of a journey in the kingdom of Kongo in central Africa.) (Naples, 1962), which discusses his failure, and the failure of the papacy, to curb excesses in slave trading at Catholic missions in the Kongo kingdom.

216 **A history of the American Board Missions in Angola, 1880-1940.**
Fola Soremekun. PhD thesis, Northwestern University, Evanston, Illinois, 1965. (Available from University Microfilms, Ann Arbor, Michigan, order no. 66-2744).

Provides a detailed history of Protestant missionary activity in Angola. In the introduction, the existing pattern of Umbundu social and political life is outlined. Subsequent chapters deal with the establishment of the missions, the growth of their educational activities, and their political significance in the colony.

217 **Misiones capuchinas em Africa. Vol 1: La mision del Congo** (Capuchin missions in Africa. Vol 1: The Congo mission.)
(Padre) Juan Garcia Mateo de Anguiano, edited and introduced by Buenaventura de Carrocera. Madrid: Consejo Superior de Investigaciones Científicas, Instituto Santo Toribio de Mogrovejo, 1950. 494p. maps. (Biblioteca «Missionalia Hispánica», no. 7).

First of three books written by the Spanish Capuchin priest, Padre Mateo de Anguiano (1649-1726), which describe his missionary activities in the Congo in the 17th and 18th centuries.

218  **Monumenta missionaria Africana: Africa occidental.** (African
     missionary activity: West Africa.)
     (Padre) António Brasio.  Lisbon: Agência Geral do Ultramar, 1952-
     89. 20 vols.

This mammoth collection includes all the briefer extant documents relating to
Portuguese missionary activity in West Africa from the late 15th through to the early
17th centuries. The work is organised chronologically, and in the course of two series
(fifteen volumes in the first, five in the second), covers over 4,000 separate documents.
Annotations are provided, along with references to the archives in Angola and
Portugal in which the originals are stored.

219  **One hundred years of Christian mission in Angola and Zaire, 1878-1978.**
     London: Baptist Missionary Society, 1978, 50p. map.

This 'centenary brochure' reviews the activities of the Baptist Missionary Society of the
UK in Angola and Zaïre since 1878. After greetings from the General Secretaries of
the Baptist Church in each country, Clifford Parsons provides an historical overview of
Baptist involvement in recent events, including its position on the guerilla struggle
since 1961. Finally, a detailed review is made of the situation in particular provinces.

220  **La pratique missionnaire des PP. Capucins italiens dans les royaumes de
     Congo, Angola, et contrées adjacents, brièvement exposée pour éclairer
     et guider les missionnaires destinés a ces saintes missions.** (The
     missionary practice of the Italian Capuchin friars in the kingdoms of
     Congo, Angola and neighbouring countries, briefly expounded to
     enlighten and guide missionaries destined to these sacred missions.)
     Hyacinthe de Bologne, translated from the Italian by Jacques
     Nothumb.  Louvain, Belgium: Editions de l'Aucam, 1931. 188p.
     (Collection de la Section Scientifique de l'Aucam, no. 2).

A translation of texts written by the Italian Capuchin friar, Hyacinthe de Bologne in
the 18th century. They cover his voyage to, and arrival in, Luanda, and then focus on
the daily life of a missionary. Included are instructions on how to live correctly, and
administer the sacraments, as well as observations on the good and bad customs of the
Congolese and Angolans. The original Italian text, first published in 1747, is printed
alongside the French translations. The documents themselves form part of the Congo
Archives of the then *Institut Royal Colonial* in Brussels.

221  **The social responses of Christianity in Angola: selected issues.**
     Thomas Masaji Okuma.  Boston, Massachussets: Boston University
     Press, 1964. 277p. bibliog.

An historical account, which divides mission activity in Angola into the age of
discovery; the era of the slave trade; intensified missionary work (since 1865); and
finally the Salazar era.

## Religion

222 **State and the church in Angola 1450-1980.**
Gerhard Grohs, Godehard Czernik. Geneva: Institut Universitaire de Hautes Études Internationales, 1983. 100p. maps. bibliog. (International Studies on Contemporary Africa, no. 3).
A brief history of the Catholic Church in Angola, which focuses on the complex ties between church and state, and attempts to explain how Christian principles became merged with colonial aims. The final chapter considers the prospects for the Church coming to terms with the separation of church and state in independent Angola, and examines the challenge of secular ideologies.

**L'ancien Congo d'après les archives romaines (1518-1640).** (The ancient Kongo according to Roman archives [1518-1640].)
*See* item no. 73.

**Cry, Angola!**
*See* item no. 250.

**The divining basket of the Ovimbundu.**
*See* item no. 505.

**Les symboles divinatoires: analyse socio-culturelle d'une technique de divination des Cokwe d'Angola (Ngombo ya Cisuka).** (Divining symbols: socio-cultural analysis of a technique for prophecy of the Chokwe of Angola [Ngombo ya Cisuka].)
*See* item no. 510.

**Portugal em Africa. Revista de Cultura Missionária.** (Portugal in Africa. Journal of Missionary Culture.)
*See* item no. 541.

# Social Conditions

**223  Angola: an appeal for prompt action to protect human rights.**
Amnesty International.    London: Amnesty International, May 1992.
13p.
After outlining the human rights provisions in the 1991 peace accords between the government and UNITA, cases of politically-motivated killings and other human rights violations since that date are documented, and a call made for an end to such human rights abuses.

**224  Angola: the real story.**
P. K. Huibregtse, translated from the Afrikaans by Nicolette Buhr.
The Hague: Forum, 1973.
Written as a combination of travel book and social and political comment, this book argued that there was no exploitation in Angola under Portuguese rule. Soon overtaken by events, it was one of the last English-language accounts favourable to the Portuguese 'mission' in Africa.

**225  Angola: violations of the laws of war by both sides.**
Jenera Rone.    London, New York: Africa Watch, 1989. 148p.
After providing a background to the civil war in Angola, this report documents the indiscriminate use of land mines, taking of hostages, targetted killings, attacks on food supplies and restrictions on the civilian populations in areas controlled by the government and UNITA respectively. In spite of its title, the report is particularly critical of conditions in UNITA-held areas, and calls for an end to US support of the organization. It also sets out relevant treaties and statutes of international law.

226 **Angolan women building the future: from national liberation to women's emancipation.**
Organization of Angolan Women, translated by Marga Holness.
London: Zed, 1984. 151p.

Contains a report of the First Congress of the Organization of Angolan Women (OMA), held in 1983. The Congress produced an open discussion of the role of women in Angolan society, and proposals to improve the situation of women. Three chapters address the general issues of women's emancipation; working women; and women and the family. The second part of the book then presents speeches at the Congress by the Angolan President, and a member of the MPLA Central Committee; also a report of the national committee of the OMA, and the resolutions and statutes of the OMA agreed at the Congress.

227 **La femme en Angola: rapport de la République Populaire d'Angola à la conférence sur la décennie des Nations Unies sur la femme.** (Women in Angola: contribution of the People's Republic of Angola to the United Nations Decade for Women.)
Luanda: República Popular de Angola, 1985. [66p.]

Contains a description of legislation affecting women's rights in the fields of nationality, electoral law, work, family, and international conventions. It then discusses women's role in development, education, and health, and the situation of refugee women in Angola. The text is in French and Portuguese.

228 **The long road home: Angola's post-war inheritance.**
J. Stephen Morrison. Washington, DC: American Council for Nationalities Service, 1991. 24p. bibliog.

Assesses the prospects for reconstruction in Angola, including problems of landmine clearance, demobilization, and the return of refugees. The paper suggests that the United Nations Special Relief Program for Angola (SRPA) has failed adequately to target humanitarian assistance, in particular in relation to various groups of displaced peoples.

229 **Organização da Mulher Angolana (OMA)/Organisation of Angolan Women/Organisation de la Femme Angolaise.**
Luanda: República Popular de Angola, 1985. [12p.]

Published with the assistance of the British non-governmental organization, War on Want, this pamphlet provides an introduction to the OMA, as well as a short description of the position of women in Angolan society. The text is in Portuguese, English and French.

230 **The people in power: an account from Angola's Second War of National Liberation.**
Ole Gjerstad. Oakland, California: LSM Press, 1977. 2nd ed. 110p.

An account of social and economic conditions in the MPLA-controlled areas of Angola during the post-independence struggle for power, based on the author's travels during 1975 and 1976. The book focuses on the growth of worker and peasant consciousness in Luanda and the Malanje provinces, as well as the role of the MPLA as a vanguard socialist party. Three appendices provide translations of interviews with senior MPLA figures, although the interview with Nito Alves, leader of the attempted coup of May 1977, which appeared in a first edition, is replaced in this edition by an interview with MPLA Secretary, Lucio Lara.

231 **Poverty and food insecurity in Luanda.**
William Bender, Simon Hunt. Luanda: UNICEF, 1991. 68p. (The Luanda Household Budget and Nutrition Survey, Working Paper no. 1).
One of six working papers prepared by the Food Studies Group at Oxford University, based on the Luanda Household Budget and Nutrition Survey of 1990. The first, and largest, paper in the series, describes the extent and intensity of poverty in Luanda after years of civil war, and identifies three groups of concern: the poor, the extremely poor, and those vulnerable to poverty. The aim is to provide a profile of poverty and vulnerability, which can be used in the formulation of economic policies, in order to maintain a 'safety net' for the poor during the period of structural adjustment. Subsequent papers in the series examine in detail the options for the alleviation of poverty, options for streamlining consumer subsidies, and the need for poverty monitoring systems to be instituted. They form a unique source of accurate recent information about social conditions in Angola, and are available from the authors.

232 **Savimbi's Angola.**
Cloete Breytenbach. Cape Town: Howard Timmins, 1980. 140p. map.
A book of photographs, taken by the South African, Cloete Breytenbach, which provide a vivid portrait of life in the UNITA-held areas of Angola in the latter part of the 1970s.

233 **Situation analysis of children and women in Angola.**
Simon Hunt. Oxford: Food Studies Group, 1992. 123p.
This report on the position of women and children in Angola is based on recent field research funded by UNICEF. It is available from the author, at the Food Studies Group, Queen Elizabeth House, 21 St Giles, Oxford, OX1 3LA, UK.

234 **Social change in Angola.**
Edited by Franz-Wilhelm Heimer. Munich: Weltforum, 1973. 284p. maps. bibliog. (Arnold-Bergstraesser-Institut: Material zu Entwicklung und Politik, no. 4).
This volume contains nine chapters based on original research by leading social and political scientists and historians on Angolan society. The first three chapters concentrate on the historical processes of transformation and resistance resulting from Portuguese penetration of the country. Following this, two chapters deal with the rural societies of the Cunene region and the central highlands respectively, whilst a further chapter by the editor considers cultural and economic factors affecting the social situation of the southern Ovimbundu. Finally, two chapters examine social conditions in urban and suburban Luanda, whilst the last chapter deals with European settlement in the 20th century.

235 **The social dimension of adjustment in Angola.**
Richard Pierce.   Luanda: UNICEF, 1989. 63p. bibliog.

This recent report examines the impact of structural adjustment and the economic reform programme on markets and institutions, and also on the poor of Angola at household level. The latter analysis includes identification of three vulnerable groups in Angolan society: the displaced, the 'rural affected', and the urban destitute, and considers policies to safeguard their economic position. The report is available from the author at the Food Studies Group, Queen Elizabeth House, 21 St Giles, Oxford, OX1 3LA.

236 **Status report on the emergency situation in Africa as of 15 July 1987.**
Washington, DC: United Nations Director for Emergencies in Africa, 1987. 70p.

Pages 9-24 of this report provide a fairly detailed background to destabilization and displacement of the population in Angola, as well as outlining the need for assistance in the fields of food, health, water and agriculture by the United Nations.

237 **The war in Angola: internal conditions for peace and recovery.**
Inge Tvedten.   Uppsala, Sweden: Scandinavian Institute of African Studies, 1989. 14p. (Current African Issues, no. 7).

Examines political structures, economic options and constraints, and socio-economic conditions in Angola, arguing that severe internal constraints to recovery exist, in spite of the end to the war and external aggression.

238 **Witness from the frontline: agression and resistance in southern Africa.**
Edited by Ben Turok.   London: Institute for African Alternatives, 1990. 168p.

Deals with continuing struggles throughout southern Africa, with a number of chapters focusing mainly or partly on Angola. These include papers on the effect of war on women and children; the economic effects of the war; economic restructuring; and the background to the current Angolan agreement, as well as a five page 'country profile', detailing social conditions inside the country.

**The myth and reality of Portuguese rule in Angola: a study of racial domination.**
*See* item no. 116.

**Angola beloved.**
*See* item no. 209.

**Angola: politics, economics and society.**
*See* item no. 263.

**Portuguese colonialism in Africa: the end of an era. The effects of Portuguese colonialism on education, science, culture and information.**
*See* item no. 444.

# Social Services, Health and Welfare

239 **Acta Medica Angolana.** (Angolan Medical Annals.)
Luanda: Faculdade de Medicina da Universidade de Angola, 1982- .
annual.
A scholarly, though somewhat irregular medical journal which publishes the results of
scientific investigations by teachers at the Faculty of Medicine in the University of
Angola. Most articles are in Portuguese, and focus on diseases and their treatment in
Angola.

240 **Famine and disease in the history of Angola, c.1830-1930.**
Jill Dias. *Journal of African History*, vol. 22, no. 3 (1981), p. 349-78.
A history of famine and disease in Angola that explores the connections between
irregular rainfall and lowered resistance to disease and epidemics, such as smallpox. It
is argued that the demographic and economic changes of the 19th century led to
worsening famines, and that these weakened African ability to organize resistance to
Portuguese military conquest.

241 **Medicine in the service of colonialism: medical care in Portuguese
Africa, 1885-1974.**
Martin Frederick Shapiro.   PhD thesis, University of California, Los
Angeles, 1983.
Argues that medical care was a tool of domination and social control under Portuguese
colonialism. The thesis provides a critical assessment of Portuguese efforts to improve
health care after the Second World War, including vaccination campaigns. A case
study is made of attempts to reduce trypanosomiasis (sleeping-sickness), whilst the
economics of health care are also examined.

## Social Services, Health and Welfare

242 **Programa nacional de cuidados primários de saúde. Vol. 1: Guia para o melhoramento dos abestecimentos de água em zonas rurais.** (National programme of primary health care. Vol. 1: Guide for the improvement of water supplies in rural zones.)
Ministério de Saúde. Luanda: República Popular de Angola, 1986. 54p. bibliog.

The first of six reports financed by the Swedish International Development Agency, covering various aspects of primary health care in Angola. It summarizes the problems associated with poor water, and then outlines the measures required to improve supplies, and educate and involve the community in developing clean water. Subsequent volumes deal with the treatment of a number of common diseases, the construction of pit latrines, and the elaboration of a vaccination programme. Each outlines the proposed measures to be undertaken in Angola, with the support of international aid agencies.

243 **Revista Médica de Angola.** (Medical Journal of Angola.)
Lisbon: Agência Geral das Colónias, 1921-28. annual.

A short-lived periodical publication of the Health and Hygiene Service of the colonial government, of historical interest for its medical reports on the colony. Articles are in French and Portuguese.

**Trabalho. Boletim do Instituto do Trabalho, Previdência e Acção Social.** (Employment. Bulletin of the Institute of Employment, Social Security and Social Work.)
*See* item no. 424.

# Politics

## Colonial

244 **Angola in flames.**
Kerelam Madhu Pannikar.    London: Asia Publishing House, 1962.
127p.
Written from both an Indian and a left-wing perspective, this book analyses the
background to Portuguese colonialism in Africa, and the nature of colonial rule and
African reaction to it since the 1961 rebellion. Further chapters focus on the role of the
United Nations, Portuguese policy in Mozambique, and provide an analysis of
appropriate foreign policy responses for India concerning the two colonies after the
liberation of Goa.

245 **Angola under the Portuguese: the myth and the reality.**
Gerald J. Bender.    London: Heinemann Educational, 1978. 287p.
maps. bibliog.
A study of colonial Angola which examines the role of 'Lusotropicalism', the notion
that Portuguese culture and society was uniquely non-racial. It considers the
characteristics of Portuguese settlement and rule, and the nature of interations
between Portuguese and Africans from the 15th century up to independence,
highlighting the gap between rhetoric and reality. An example was the spectacular
failure of the Portuguese policy of colonizing Angola with poor Portuguese peasants.
Bender estimates that US $100 million was spent on this policy in the last twenty years
of Portuguese rule alone. Conflicts between settlers and the indigenous populations
abounded. Inadequate selection of the settlers, or *colonatos*, and a lack of technical
assistance, are also blamed in part for the failure of the policy.

246 **Angola: a symposium. Views of a revolt.**
Institute of Race Relations, with an introduction by Philip Mason.
London: Oxford University Press, 1962. 160p. maps.

Contains ten articles, some by leading supporters, but mostly by opponents, of Portuguese rule in Angola, written for a symposium soon after the 1961 uprising. They include reflections on Portuguese rule itself, as well as background material on the revolt and Angola politics, and two chapters on relations between Portugal and Britain.

247 **Angola: five centuries of Portuguese exploitation.**
Américo Boavida. Richmond, British Columbia: Liberation Support Movement Information Center, 1972. 124p.

An important Marxist-Leninist account of Portuguese conquest and colonial rule in Angola, fully documented from Portuguese sources, and written by a prominent Angolan nationalist. In four parts, it deals separately with the political, historic, economic and international contexts to colonial society. In particular, it highlights the economic importance of Angola to Portugal, and argues that this underlay the determination of the fascist government not to grant independence. This is one of the most substantial nationalist accounts of Portuguese rule in Angola, and was first published in 1967 as *Angola: cinco séculos de exploração portuguesa* (Rio de Janeiro: Civilização Brasileira), although a semi-clandestine edition was published in Morocco in 1966. The English edition includes a Liberation Support Movement interview with the author, a tribute to him by the MPLA executive committee, and a poem dedicated to him after his death in 1969. The work has also been translated into German.

248 **Angola: repression and revolt in Portuguese Africa.**
Homer A. Jack. New York: American Committee on Africa, 1960. 28p.

An early and basic introduction to the reasons for revolt in Angola, aimed at informing the American people about conditions in the colony.

249 **Autonomia de Angola.** (Angolan autonomy.)
José de Macedo. Lisbon: Centro de Socio-Economia, Instituto de Investigação Científica Tropical, 1988. 2nd ed. 278p.

A facsimile of the original edition of 1910, published with a preface by Jorge Borges de Macedo. This work is of some significance, representing one of the more forceful calls from the settler community for autonomy in the colony of Angola. The author argues that on the basis of its distinctive environment and history, Angola's ties to metropolitan Portugal should be loosened, and power devolved to white settlers. Statistical material is presented to back up this argument.

250 **Cry, Angola!**
Len Addicott. London: SCM Press, 1962. 144p.

An account of Portuguese oppression in colonial Angola, and the attempts of the Baptist church in the United Kingdom and America to bring it to world attention after the uprising of 1961. The book is addressed to a Christian audience, and draws on the author's personal experience, as well as that of other protestant missionaries in the country.

251 **The future in Angola.**
George Martelli. London: Congo Africa, 1962. 24p.
A short pamphlet which praises the Portuguese presence in Angola, and criticises foreign supporters of 'terrorist movements'. These foreign supporters include independent African states, the Communist Bloc, and the Baptist Missionary Societies of the United States and Britain.

252 **Government-in-exile versus government-in-insurgency: the case of Angola.**
John Marcum. In: *Governments-in-exile in contemporary world politics.* Edited by Yossi Shain. New York: Routledge, 1991, p. 42-51.
A discussion of the political activities of the three insurgent movements in colonial Angola, the MPLA, UPA and UNITA, which focuses on the contrasting strategies of 'government' of these organizations. Whilst the UPA established a government-in-exile in Kinshasha, UNITA rejected exile, but sought to exercise government-like functions within insurgent-held zones, although without pretending to hold official government status. Ultimately, neither organization could beat the mixed strategy of the MPLA, which built up both a local base in 'liberated' areas, and sought strong external support through 'diplomatic' activity.

253 **Local and community power in Angola.**
Norman Bailey. *Western Political Quarterly*, vol. 21, no. 3, (Sept. 1968), p. 400-09.
Examines the process of decision making at a local level in colonial Angola, with particular reference to urban planning in the *muceques*, or shanty towns of Luanda. It is suggested that interest groups did have the means to influence decision-makers, although for some in the shanties, this meant a necessity to resort to violence.

254 **Portugal's stand in Africa.**
Adriano Moreira. New York: University Publishers, 1962. 219p.
A defence of Portugal's African policy by the Ministry for the Overseas Provinces. The author criticises French, Belgian and British colonial régimes, before advocating a 'hearts and minds' campaign to maintain African confidence in Portugal's territories.

**Angola: the real story.**
*See* item no. 224.

**Portuguese colonialism from South Africa to Europe.**
*See* item no. 374.

# Post-independence

**255 L'Afrique en guerre: Tchad, Ethiopie, Sahara Occidental, Angola.**
(Africa at war: Chad, Ethiopia, Western Sahara, Angola.)
London: Service Français de la BBC, 1987. 193p.

Consists of transcriptions of eight BBC World Service radio broadcasts from Angola between August-September 1987. All are in French. The programmes provided an opportunity for both the government and UNITA to put their point of view on the history of the Angolan conflict, economic, political and military considerations, and the prospects for peace. The programmes were assembled by Jean-Victor Nkolo in Luanda, and Laurence Lalanne for UNITA.

**256 Afro-marxist régimes: ideology and public policy.**
Edited by Edmond J. Keller, Donald Rothschild. Boulder, Colorado; London: Lynne Rienner, 1987. 335p.

This volume on African marxist régimes is organized in three parts, focusing respectively on ideology and the consolidation of state power; the policy-making process; and international influences on state policy. In each part there is a chapter on Angola: thus Chapter 4 by John Marcum (p. 67-84) outlines the lack of ideological flexibility of the MPLA, and calls into question the party's ability to achieve peaceful development of the country; Chapter 8 by Gillian Gunn (p. 181-98) analyses the contradictions between Angola's political ties with the Eastern Bloc, and its continuing technological and economic dependence on the West; whilst Chapter 11 by Robert Price (p. 257-80) outlines South Africa's impact on public policy in both Angola and Mozambique. Other countries featuring in the volume include Ethiopia and Zimbabwe.

**257 After Angola: the war over southern Africa.**
Colin Legum, Tony Hodges. London: Rex Collings; New York: Africana, 1976. 85p.

This work is divided into four parts. The first two, by Colin Legum, outline the role of the Western powers in southern Africa as a whole, and then foreign intervention in Angola by the West; by the Soviet Union, China and Cuba; and also by other African states, notably Zambia. The third part, by Tony Hodges, describes the victory of the MPLA in the Second War of National Liberation, whilst also providing some data on Angola's economic and trade situation. The final part is devoted to documents that include the texts of various accords between the MPLA, UNITA and the FNLA, as well as speeches by the leaders of the three movements.

**258 Angola 1989. Reconstruction.**
Researched and edited by Daniel dos Santos, My dos Santos, Pierre Beaudet. Montreal: Centre d'Information et de Documentation sur le Mozambique et l'Afrique Australe (CIDMAA); Ottawa: Canadian Council for International Cooperation, 1990. 205p. maps. bibliog.

Provides basic facts on Angola, including a chronological list of historical events, before presenting facsimile reproductions of a number of documents relating to the peace process, UNITA, the economy, and external actors. Many of the latter are articles from US, United Kingdom and South African magazines and newspapers. All reports from

Portuguese sources are translated into English. The documents are supplemented by short editorial notes. A full bibliography on Angola, including newspaper articles published in the 1980s, is provided on p. 193-205.

259 **Angola in the front line.**
Michael Wolfers, Jane Bergerol.   London: Zed Press, 1983. 238p.
maps. bibliog.
An account of events in Angola since independence written by two journalists with first hand experience of the conflict between the MPLA and various internal and external forces. The book examines the war of 1975-76, the subsequent power struggle within the MPLA, and finally the attempts of the Movement to rebuild the country on socialist lines in the late 1970s and early 1980s. Emphasis is placed both on the nature and extent of external aggression, and especially the role of South Africa and the United States in destabilizing the country since independence. In the second half of the book, there is more detailed consideration of the inner workings of the MPLA itself.

260 **The Angola/Namibia accords.**
Chas W. Freeman Jr.   *Foreign Affairs*, vol. 68, no. 3 (summer 1989), p. 126-41.
A discussion of the background to the Angola/Namibia accords signed in New York in 1988, which includes an assessment of the motives of each of the main parties, South Africa, Cuba, and Angola, in signing them.

261 **Angola revisited.**
David Birmingham.   *Journal of Southern African Studies*, vol. 15, no. 1 (Oct. 1988), p. 1-14.
An impressionistic account of continuity rather than transformation in post-independence Angola, based on a return trip to the country by the author in 1987. Themes of continuity cited include authoritarianism, civil war between city and countryside, foreign war, and a thriving black market.

262 **Angola: one step to peace in southern Africa.**
Stuart Northolt.   London: Bow Group, 1988. 30p.
This pamphlet argues for British involvement to end the stalemate in Angola and promote negotiations between the Luanda government and UNITA. It includes a resumé of the history of foreign intervention in the country, and of the progress of the civil war and negotiations.

263 **Angola: politics, economics and society.**
Ken Somerville.   London: Frances Pinter; Boulder, Colorado: Lynne Rienner, 1986. 207p. bibliog. (Marxist Régimes Series).
This book charts the post-Revolutionary experience of Angola under the MPLA, and its attempts to reconstruct the Angolan society and economy despite continuing civil war. A brief history of the pre-colonial and colonial periods is followed by more detailed analysis of the liberation struggle, and the political, economic and social systems of Angola since independence.

264 **Angola: rumo à independência. O governo de transição: documentos e personalidades.** (Angola: path to independence. The transitional government: documents and personalities.)
Edited by Carmo Vaz.   Luanda: Livrangol [1975]. 212p.

A collection of documents relating to the transitional government in 1975. After an introduction to the independence struggle, two chapters present various documents relating to the Mombasa and Alvor Accords. These are followed by speeches and profiles of members of the transitional government from all three 'parties'. In Chapters 5 and 6, there are translations into English and French of the speech of Jomo Kenyatta at Mombasa; the text of the Alvor Accord; the text of a speech by the Portuguese minister responsible for decolonization, António de Almeida Santos; and a short message to the Angolan people by Manuel Rui Monteiro, the first Minister for Information of the transitional government. These English translations are by Michael Chapman.

265 **Angola: the struggle continues.**
Marga Holness.   In: *Destructive engagement: southern Africa at war*.
Edited by Phyllis Johnston, David Martin.   Harare: Zimbabwe Publishing House, 1986, p. 73-109.

Provides a concise account of destabilization in Angola, outlining the nature of the liberation struggle, and stressing UNITA's links with Portuguese military intelligence, before emphasizing both United States and South African involvement in the continuing conflict in Angola after independence.

266 **L'Angola: un défi.** (Angola: a challenge.)
Edited by Bernard Couret.   Paris: Berger Levrault, 1987. 64p. bibliog.

A booklet containing reprints of a number of interesting articles on Angola published in *Le Monde Diplomatique* in 1986. All were revised for this edition. They cover political, historical, economic and cultural aspects of the crisis, and provide an interesting journalistic introduction to the country.

267 **The battle for Angola, 1974-1988: a set back for communism in Africa.**
Branko Lazitch, in collaboration with Pierre Rigoulot, translated from the French by Nicholas Rowe.   London: Better Britain Society, 1989. 70p. map.

A right-wing account of the MPLA government and the support for it from the Soviet Union and Cuba. The author argues that MPLA rule has led to economic disaster and military near-defeat, despite massive Soviet aid. First published as *Angola, 1974-1988: un échec du communisme en Afrique* (Paris: Est & West, 1988).

268 **Cabinda: the politics of oil in Angola's enclave.**
Daniel dos Santos.   In: *African islands and enclaves*. Edited by Robin Cohen.   London; Beverly Hills, California: Sage, 1983, p. 101-18.

Discusses the historical background to the incorporation of Cabinda into the colony of Angola, and the overwhelming economic and strategic case for independent Angola to wish to continue to rule the territory. There is also a section of the development of the oil economy in Cabinda, and on the rise of 'liberation' movements seeking independence for the enclave.

269 **The challenge to the MPLA: Angola's war, 1980-1986.**
James Hamill. Coventry, England: University of Warwick, 1986. 74p.
(University of Warwick, Department of Politics, Working Paper
no. 41).

An analysis of the threat posed to the MPLA government by UNITA. Includes a
discussion of the progress of the war, UNITA's political stance, and foreign
interventions in the war on behalf of both the government and the rebels.

270 **The conflict resolution process in Angola.**
Anthony G. Pazzanita. *Journal of Modern African Studies*, vol. 29,
no. 1 (March 1991), p. 83-114.

Discusses the background to the 1988 New York accords, examining the causes of the
Angolan conflict, and its intractability. Emphasis is placed in particular on the Angolan
offensive on Mavinga in August 1987, and the South African/UNITA counter-offensive
and siege of Cuito Cuanavale starting in December the same year. The article argues
that these military events were so extraordinary in scale and nature as to convince all
parties that prompt settlement of the conflict was the only viable option.

271 **The decolonization conflict in Angola, 1974-76: an essay in political
sociology.**
F. W. Heimer. Geneva: Institut Universitaire de Hautes Etudes
Internationales, 1979. 117p. bibliog. (International Studies on
Contemporary Africa, no. 2).

A short monograph on the background to decolonization, which starts from the
premise that the events of 1974-76 were fundamentally conditioned by the nature of
Angolan society, rather than being determined by external forces, as is often assumed.
On this basis, the book outlines the structure of Angolan society that had been created
by colonialism, and then presents five models of decolonization, which emerged in
political debates after the Portuguese coup of 1974. Different phases of the 1974-76
period are then explained as resulting from the struggle between these models, and the
result of the conflict for Angolan society is assessed.

272 **Diplomacy and the Angola/Namibia accords.**
Geoff R. Berridge. *International Affairs*, vol. 65, no. 3 (summer
1989), p. 463-79.

Examines in detail the process of negotiation in the New York talks on Namibia and
Angola in late 1988. The author argues that diplomatic procedures, particularly the
linkage of disputes in the two countries, and the mediating and guarantor role of the
United States, contributed to the talks' successful conclusion.

273 **Lusophone Africa: Angola, Mozambique and Guinea-Bissau.**
Thomas H. Henriksen. In: *Politics and government in African states,
1960-1985*. Edited by Peter Duignan, R. H. Jackson. London,
Sydney: Croom Helm, 1986, p. 377-407.

Provides an introduction to the government, economy and post-independence
institutions of Angola, comparing these with Mozambique and Guinea-Bissau.

274 **The 1988 peace accords and the future of south western Africa.**
Robert S. Jaster. London: Brassey's, for the Interntional Institute for
Strategic Studies, 1990. 76p. maps. (Adelphi Papers, no. 253).
Begins with a detailed account of the wars in Angola and Namibia from 1977-90. After
a brief introduction to the history of the two countries, the author describes the
escalation first of a bush war, and subsequently of a conventional conflict between
South Africa and SWAPO on the one hand, and the South African backed forces of
UNITA and the Angolan army on the other. He then goes on to analyse the events
that led to the signing of the peace settlement in Namibia, and the prospects for peace
in the region as a whole. He argues that although the 1988 peace accords and the
realignment of South Africa's foreign and domestic policy have helped to reduce the
number and intensity of conflicts in the region, it was the political changes in the Soviet
Union, and especially the redefinintion of Soviet foreign policy, which were the major
catalysts for change. This resulted from the fact that southern Africa as a whole has
now become less significant in geopolitical terms for the two superpowers.

275 **Peacemaking in southern Africa: the Luanda-Pretoria tug of war.**
Gerald J. Bender. *Third World Quarterly*, vol. 11 (April 1989),
p. 15-30.
Discusses the progress of the Angolan conflict to 1988, and events in that year in
particular which led to changes in Angolan, Cuban and South African policy. The
author suggests that it was a change in South African attitudes to Namibia which
allowed the crucial breakthrough which led to the signing of the New York peace
accord.

276 **People's war, state formation, and revolution in Africa: a comparative
analysis of Mozambique, Guinea-Bissau and Angola.**
Patrick Chabal. *Journal of Commonwealth and Comparative Politics*,
vol. 21, no. 3 (Nov. 1983), p. 104-25.
Considers the argument that the process of people's war in Angola, Mozambique and
Guinea-Bissau led to favourable conditions for fundamental change in political, social
and economic structures, and the growth of a revolutionary state. Chabal sees Angola
as strong enough economically to pursue an independent political stance, and he
accepts that the period of people's war did have a fundamental influence on subsequent
policy. However, the article goes on to argue that there were still only weak prospects
for revolutionary transformation even in Angola, for a number of reasons.

277 **Political development in Afro-Marxist régimes: an analysis of Angola
and Mozambique.**
Catherine V. Scott. PhD thesis, Emory University, Atlanta, Georgia,
1986. (Available from University Microfilms, Ann Arbor, Michigan,
order no. 8629856).
Explains the process of political development in Angola and Mozambique after
independence with reference to 'African Socialist' and 'Marxist-Leninist' models.
Through an analysis of party administration, agrarian policy, and civil-military
relations, it is argued that both countries conform to the former model, with little
evidence of 'revolutionary breakthrough'.

278 **A political history of the civil war in Angola, 1974-1990.**
W. Martin James III.   New Brunswick, New Jersey: Transaction,
1991. 314p. bibliog. (East-South Relations Series).

An account of the civil war which cites, 'personal jealousy, contrasting ideologies and
ethnic animosities' as its main causes. The book argues that the Reagan Doctrine of
support to insurgent movements such as UNITA was successful in forcing a Cuban
withdrawal from Angola. Individual chapters focus on the internal organization of
UNITA and the extent of its popular support; as well as the movement's internal
cohesion, its external support, and the response of the MPLA government.

279 **Socialism and the 'soft state' in Africa: an analysis of Angola and
Mozambique.**
Catherine Scott.   *Journal of Modern African Studies*, vol. 26, no. 1
(March 1988), p. 23-36.

Argues that Angola has displayed a number of characteristics of a 'soft state' since
independence, despite an ideological commitment to 'scientific socialism'. These
include nepotism, corruption, factionalism, purges and political conspiracy.

280 **Southern African Record.**
Braamfontein, South Africa: South African Institute of International
Affairs, 1975- . quarterly.

Publishes the original texts and abstracts from statements by political leaders,
government representatives and international organizations concerned with international relations within the region. During the 1980s, a number of texts relating to the
New York agreement on Angola/Namibia, and statements of the Angolan government
to the UN Security Council were included.

281 **The war for Africa: twelve months that transformed a continent.**
Fred Bridgland.   Gibraltar: Ashanti, 1990. 403p.

An account of the Angolan conflict, based on interviews with ordinary South African
soldiers who fought during the campaigns of 1987/88 in southern Angola. A journalistic
account, the book contains numerous photographs, and diagrams of battle
manoeuvres.

282 **War in Angola: the final South African phase.**
Helmoed-Römer Heitman.   Gibraltar: Ashanti, 1990. 366p. maps.

Focuses on the operations of a small force (about 3,000 men) of South African
soldiers, who fought alongside UNITA in 1987-88. The book argues that the success of
this 'carefully applied and directed force' changed the course of the war, and led to the
peace negotiations. Detailed descriptions are provided of the military operations
involving the South Africans, although no information is provided about other UNITA
activities.

**Witness from the frontline: agression and resistance in southern Africa.**
*See* item no. 238.

**Angola, 11 de Novembro de 1975. Documentos da independência/Documents de l'independence/Documents of Independency.** (Angola, 11 November 1975: Documents of independence.)
*See* item no. 310.

**Politics in modern Africa: the uneven tribal dimension.**
*See* item no. 328.

# MPLA

283 **Agostinho Neto.**
A. M. Khazanov, translated from the Russian by Cynthia Carlile.
Moscow: Progress Publishers, 1986. 302p.
This biography of the poet, doctor, and leader of the MPLA, Agostinho Neto, from his first voyage to Portugal in 1947 to his death in Moscow in 1979, concentrates on his political career, which culminated, according to the author, with the MPLA's formal adoption of Marxism-Leninism in 1977. Extracts from some of Neto's poems are included in a full and sympathetic account of his life.

284 **All roads lead to Angola: in solidarity with the struggle of the Angolan people/MPLA.**
Cairo: Permanent Secretariat of the AAPSO, 1976. [n.p.]
(Afro-Asian Publications, no. 71).
A collection of appeals on behalf of the MPLA, press releases, reports of missions, and resolutions, all passed or approved by the AAPSO in 1975/76.

285 **Angola in Arms.**
Lusaka: MPLA, 1967-72. monthly.
The newsletter of the MPLA published during the liberation struggle, which included information on the progress of the armed insurrection, reports on foreign support for the MPLA, and occasional articles on Angolan culture and society.

286 **Angola in struggle.**
Supplement to *Journal on Social Change and Development*,
(May 1988). 13p. maps.
Produced in association with the Angolan Embassy in Harare, this supplement provides basic background information on the armed struggle in Angola, as well as a portrait of life in the country under MPLA rule.

287 **Angola in the whirlwind of permanent revolution.**
Claude Gabriel. *Africa in Struggle*, special issue (1976), 39p.

Contains six articles, five by the author, and one by F. Cazals, which analyse the political situation in post-independence Angola from a revolutionary Marxist perspective. They argue that only by breaking from the imperialist world economy, as well as the bureacracies of the USSR and China, can Angola truly develop and prioritize social goals.

288 **Angola na reconstrução nacional.** (Angola in national reconstruction.)
Anon [MPLA: no date or publisher given]. 112p.

A book of photographs commemorating the first years of Angolan independence under the MPLA. There is an introduction and commentary in English, as well as in Portuguese, French and German.

289 **Angola: documentos do MPLA.** (Angola: documents of the MPLA.)
Edited by José Fortunato. Lisbon: Ulmeiro, 1977. 254p. (3º Mundo e Revolução, Série 2).

Contains various documents in Portuguese by and about the MPLA prior to the achievement of independence, including interviews with MPLA leaders, MPLA broadsheets, newspaper articles, and radio broadcasts, and messages and announcements made by the Party to the people.

290 **Angolan socialism.**
Kevin Brown. In: *Socialism in sub-Saharan Africa: a new assessment.*
Edited by Carl G. Rosberg, Thomas M. Callaghy. Berkeley, California: Institute of International Studies, University of California, 1979, p. 296-321.

This discussion of MPLA policy after independence stresses differences from other African socialist parties, and the crucial role of the leader of the African revolt in Guinea-Bissau, Amílcar Cabral, in influencing ideological debate in the party. The failure of attempts to mobilize grassroots support, however, is seen as the cause of continued factionalism inside the MPLA. Problems engendered by the civil war are also considered.

291 **Boletim do Militante.** (Militant's Bulletin.)
Luanda: MPLA, 1977-79. monthly.

An information bulletin for party activists of the MPLA, containing news and reports on political issues.

292 **Discursos do Camarada Presidente José Eduardo dos Santos.** (Speeches of Comrade President José Eduardo dos Santos.)
Luanda: Editora Vanguarda, 1982- . quarterly.

A collection of major speeches and proclamations by the MPLA President, interrupted, but which restarted publication in 1989. This series takes over from one entitled '*Discursos do Camarada Presidente António Agostinho Neto*, published from 1978-79. Both are available at the Centro de Informação e Difusão Amílcar Cabral in Lisbon.

293 **How the Angolan revolution was built.**
Joe Slovo. *The African Communist*, vol. 74 (1978), p. 18-36.
The first part of an interview with Lúcio Lara, conducted by Joe Slovo, and first published in the Portuguese journal *Tempo* (no. 400 [1970], p. 41-48). Conversation centres on the general historical background to the Angolan conflict, Angolan nationalism, language, class structure, trades unions, and the role of traditional chiefs in post-independence society. The second part of the interview, 'The Angolan revolution: main phases in the development of the MPLA', was published in the next issue (vol. 75, [1978], p. 53-73), and covered problems of exile, the causes of the attempted coup of May 27, 1977, the armed struggle, the building of a socialist government, and relations with South Africa.

294 **Interviews in depth. Angola: MPLA.**
Liberation Support Movement (LSM). Richmond, British Columbia: LSM Press, 1973.
This series of in-depth interviews with leaders and militants of liberation movements includes four booklets on Angola. They cover interviews with Paulo Jorge, director of the MPLA's Department of Information and Propaganda, as well as Seta Likambuila, Daniel Chipenda and Spartacus Monimambu.

295 **The making of a middle cadre: the story of Rui de Pinto.**
Taped and edited by Don Barnett. Richmond, British Columbia: LSM Press, 1973. 107p. (Life Histories from the Revolution: Angola, MPLA, no. 1).
The life history of an MPLA soldier, Rui Pinto, as told to a member of the US-based Liberation Support Movement. Six chapters deal with his education, a spell in Portugal, the rebellion of 1961, and the Long March, through to his joining the MPLA's struggle for independence. The book is a vivid personal account of the anti-colonial struggle.

296 **National liberation and state power: an anarchist critique of the MPLA in Angola.**
Martin Spence. Newcastle upon Tyne, England: Black Jake Collective at Tyneside Free Press Workshop, 1977. 16p. bibliog.
A short assessment of the MPLA from an anarchist perspective, which provides a brief historical outline of the Party and its internal contradictions, as well as a review of the 'libertarian alternatives' for Angola.

297 **Road to liberation: MPLA documents on the founding of the People's Republic of Angola.**
Translated from the Portuguese by members of the Liberation Support Movement. Oakland, California: LSM Press, 1976. 52p.
A booklet containing the Independence Day speech of Agostinho Neto, the new President of the People's Republic of Angola (PRA); the speech of MPLA Secretary Lúcio Lara at the investiture of Neto as President; the flag, emblem, and anthem of the PRA; a brief history of the MPLA, and a poem dedicated to those who died in the independence struggle. All are reprinted from the Independence Day issue of the

MPLA's official newsheet, *Vitória Certa* (Certain Victory). Also included is the new constitution of independent Angola.

298 **Textos e documentos do MPLA sobre a revolução angolana.** (Texts and documents of the MPLA concerning the Angolan revolution.)
M. I. P. Ventura.   Lisbon: Edições Maria da Fonte, 1971. 117p.
(Libertação Nacional).
A collection of eleven documents, including radio broadcasts, extracts from the MPLA organ *Vitória ou Morte* (Victory or Death), messages from Agostinho Neto to the Angolan people, and a declaration of the principles of the MPLA. All are in the original Portuguese.

299 **Visit to MPLA and their liberated areas, May-September 1974.**
Gaetano Pagano.   London: International Universities Exchange Fund (IUEF), 1975. [n.p.].
A report of field research undertaken to clarify the MPLA's political programme, projects, and priorities for humanitarian assistance. Included is a description of visits by the team to the northern and eastern fronts, and recommendations for action by the IUEF. Annexes include a brief historical outline, a chronology of the events of 1974-75, and lists of MPLA aid requirements.

**The people in power: an account from Angola's Second War of National Liberation.**
*See* item no. 230.

**Angola in the front line.**
*See* item no. 259.

**1980 Angola: special congress report of the Central Committee of the MPLA-Workers Party.**
*See* item no. 322.

**People's Republic of Angola.**
*See* item no. 323.

# UNITA

300 **Account from Angola: UNITA as described by ex-participants and foreign visitors.**
William Minter.   *Facts and Reports*, (15 June 1990), p. 2-15.
An important report, which provides a detailed analysis of UNITA's operations inside Angola, based on the testimonies of ex-soldiers and others captured by UNITA.

301 **Angola: a resistência em busca de uma nova nação.** (Angola: the resistance in search of a new nation.)
Jonas Malheiro Savimbi. Lisbon: Agência Portuguesa de Revistas, 1979. 210p.

Savimbi's first book in which he outlines his own, and UNITA's political programme. Individual essays deal with the history of UNITA, the events in the aftermath of the Portuguese revolution of 1974; the need for democracy and popular participation; and UNITA's ties with the Black American community. There is also a collection of photographs, and a number of documents relating to UNITA's struggle. In a subsequent book (*Por um futuro melhor.* [For a better future], Lisbon: Nova Nórdica, 1986), which starts with text from this volume, a number of speeches by Savimbi provide further insight into the evolution of the UNITA president's political goals from 1979-85. Both books are written mainly for an international audience, and defend UNITA's record.

302 **Hostage.**
Glen Dixon, as told to Anthony Mockler. London: Columbus, 1986. 189p.

Glen Dixon and his companions, foreign workers in the diamond-mining industry, were captured by UNITA in a raid in the province of Lunda Norte in 1984. This is a personal story of their capture, their forced march south to UNITA's headquarters, and eventual release. It provides a not-unsympathetic picture of UNITA.

303 **Jonas Savimbi: a key to Africa.**
Fred Bridgland. London: Hodder & Stoughton, 1988. 2nd ed. 671p.
(Coronet Books Series).

A sympathetic biography of Jonas Savimbi, and also an account of the civil war up to 1986, written by an English journalist working for Reuters. The book provides a limited background on Savimbi's early life and studies, as well as the struggle of the pre-Independence period. However, the bulk of the book is concerned with UNITA's war against the MPLA, and Savimbi's own search for support abroad, based on personal interviews with the UNITA leader. It is argued that UNITA and Savimbi deserve fuller support from the West.

304 **Savimbi's 1977 campaign against the Cubans and the MPLA. Observed for 7½ months, and covering 2,100 miles inside Angola.**
Leon de Costa Dash, Jr. Pasadena, California: Caltech, 1977. 116p.
(Munger African Library Notes, nos. 40-41).

An important account of the civil war in 1976/77 by an American journalist, based on an epic journey inside UNITA-held southern Angola. It describes attacks on MPLA and Cuban camps, as well as life in the UNITA zone. Though favourable to Savimbi, there are also many observations on internal problems in his movement.

305 **UNITA and ethnic nationalism in Angola.**
Linda M. Heywood. *Journal of Modern African Studies*, vol. 27
(March 1989), p. 47-66.
Examines the significance of ethnic issues in the development of UNITA, and its search for political legitimacy. After consideration of factors both internal and external to Angola, the article concludes that UNITA's link with Ovimbundu nationalism is both one of the greatest strengths of the movement, and one of its greatest weaknesses.

306 **The UNITA insurgency in Angola.**
W. Martin James. PhD thesis, Catholic University of America,
Washington, DC, 1986. (Available from University Microfilms, Ann
Arbor, Michigan, order no. 8702202).
This study desribes UNITA's organization, and outlines the basis for its popular support within Angola. It argues that contrasting ideologies, tribal animosities, and also personal ambition were important factors in generating the civil war, and that 'blame' cannot simply be placed on external intervention. Included is a full bibliography of UNITA documents, newspaper articles, congressional hearings and statements made in the US Congress on Angola.

307 **UNITA: myth and reality.**
Augusta Conchiglia, translated from the Italian and edited by Marga
Holness. London: European Campaign Against South African
Aggression on Mozambique and Angola (ECASAAMA), [n.d.]. 106p.
Detailed and critical account of UNITA's internal organization and network of external support, particularly amongst right-wing groups in Europe.

308 **UNITA: União Nacional para a Independência Total de Angola.**
(UNITA: National Union for the Total Independence of Angola.)
W. Dohning. Angola: Kwacha Unita Press, 1984. 93p.
An English-language publicity book for UNITA, containing numerous colour photographs by Cloete Breytenbach of UNITA-held areas of Angola, and short articles on UNITA's political, ideological and organizational characteristics, as well as the MPLA's mismanagement of the economy, and the necessity for external support for UNITA.

**Operation Timber: papers from the Savimbi dossier.**
*See* item no. 139.

**The cold war guerilla: Jonas Savimbi, the US media, and the Angolan war.**
*See* item no. 353.

**In search of enemies: a CIA story.**
*See* item no. 355.

# Constitution and the Legal System

309 **African customary law in the former Portuguese territories, 1954-74.**
Narana Loissoro. *Journal of African Law*, vol. 28, nos. 1-2
(spring-autumn 1984), p. 72-79.

A short article examining the status of African customary law in the former Portuguese
colonies, and Portuguese attempts to mould African customary practices to fit
European legal concepts.

310 **Angola, 11 de Novembro de 1975. Documentos da independência/**
**Documents de l'independence/Documents of Independency.** (Angola,
11 November 1975: Documents of independence.)
Edited by the Ministry of Information. Luanda: Imprensa Nacional,
1975. 164p.

A book containing seven documents relating to independence, published in
Portuguese, French and English. They are: the Proclamation of Independence; the
Constitutional Law of 1975; the investiture speech of Agostinho Neto; the Act of
Investiture; the speeches of the prime minister and president at the swearing in of the
new government; and the Nationality Law, which defines Angolan nationality.

311 **Angola–Cape Verde–Guinea–Mozambique–San Tomé and**
**Principe–Timor rural labour code.**
Geneva: International Labour Office, 1962. 87p.

This is the English text of the Rural Labour Code for the Portuguese colonies brought
into force by Decree Law 44309 in 1962. This code superceded the Indigenous Labour
Code of 1928, under which there had been widespread allegations of the continuation
of forced labour.

312    Angola: human rights guarantees in the revised constitution.
Amnesty International.    London: Amnesty International, June 1991.
33p.

An account of Amnesty International's memorandum to the National Commission for the Revision of the Constitutional Law, and subsequent amendments of the constitution relating to human rights.

313    **Folhas da Legislação da República Popular de Angola.** (Serial of Legislation of the People's Republic of Angola.)
Luanda: República Popular de Angola, 1975- . irregular.

Provides a digest of legislation passed, including a note of the existing laws that the new legislation is intended to supercede.

314    **Legislação penal revolucionária.** (Revolutionary penal legislation.)
Luanda: República Popular de Angola, 1976. 89p.

Contains the Combatants Disciplinary Code of the MPLA (1966) on rewards, decorations, and punishments; the text of an order banning capital punishment except when confirmed by the MPLA president (1970); Decree Law 3/75 which established the *Divisão de Informação e Segurança de Angola* (DISA), or state security police, in 1975; and finally Law 7/76 on revolutionary courts, passed in 1976. The text is in Portuguese, English and French.

315    **Organic law of the Portuguese overseas provinces.**
Lisbon: Agência Geral do Ultramar, 1963. 62p.

A legal framework (*lei orgánica*) of the Portuguese colonies, translated into English.

316    **Trends in Portuguese overseas legislation for Africa.**
Alfredo Héctor Wilensky, translated from the Spanish by Frank R.
Holliday.    Braga, Portugal: Editora Pax, 1971. 268p. bibliog.

An analysis of the changing legislative framework for Portuguese Africa during the period of the Salazar dictatorship. After an introductory chapter outlining legislation in force at the time of confirmation of Salazar in office, the bulk of the work examines in detail subsequent debates over its alteration. Although a paternalist element in policy-making is identified, the author argues that most impetus for changes in legislation came from outside Portugal and its colonies. A difficult translation of a legalistic account, this is little less accessible in the original Spanish (*Tendencias de la legislación ultramarina portuguesa en Africa*, Braga, Portugal: Editora Pax, 1968).

**La femme en Angola: rapport de la Republique Populaire d'Angola à la conference sur la decennie des Nations Unies sur la femme.** (Women in Angola: contribution of the People's Republic of Angola to the United Nations Decade for Women.)
*See* item no. 227.

**Constitution and the Legal System**

**Road to liberation: MPLA documents on the founding of the People's Republic of Angola.**
*See* item no. 297.

**Boletim de Informação.** (Information Bulletin.)
*See* item no. 320.

**A history of labour law in Angola.**
*See* item no. 420.

# Party and Government Administration

317 **Alguns aspectos da administração de Angola em época de reformas (1834-1851).** (Some aspects of the administration of Angola in the reform period [1834-1851].)
Mário António Fernandes de Oliveira. Lisbon: Faculdade de Ciências Sociais e Humanas, Universidade Nova de Lisboa, 1981. 367p.

A study of colonial administration in the mid 19th century. First, it examines the background to Angola at that time, singling out the importance of the slave trade, the growth of creole society, and the dominance of the private sector in the economy. Subsequently, the period of instability and conflict from the 1830s to the 1850s is discussed both in general terms, and then specifically through analyses of the legal system, the agricultural sector, and the nationalization of commerce. Conflict over the position of the naval station in Angola is also considered in some detail. Overall, the objective is to consider the impact of the reform movement in the colony, and the extent to which more general forces for economic and political change were influenced by local factors.

318 **Angola 1962-1966. Acção governativa.** (Angola 1962-1966. Government activity.)
Luanda: Imprensa Nacional, 1966-67. 2 vols.

Volume 1 contains speeches by the Governor-General, Secretary-General, and Provincial Secretaries for the Economy, Rural Development, Public Works and Communications, Health, Welfare and Social Security, and Education. Volume 2 then describes the civil administration of the colony, and aspects of health, education, the economy, civil service, and government budget. This is followed by numerous illustrated maps, tables, and plans showing the evolution of the economy and government activity during this period.

319 **ANGOP News Bulletin.**
London: Agência Angola Press, 1985-87. fortnightly.

A set of typewritten reports published for a time in London by the national Angolan news agency, ANGOP, mostly covering government announcements, official visits, etc.

320 **Boletim de Informação.** (Information Bulletin.)
Lisbon: República Popular de Angola, 1979- . monthly.

This monthly bulletin of the Angolan embassy in Lisbon covers major government proclamations, as well as important changes in Angolan law.

321 **Boletim Oficial da Província de Angola.** (Official bulletin of the Province of Angola.)
Luanda: Governo da Província de Angola, 1845-1975. daily.

The daily official bulletin of the colonial government, listing legislation, government appointments, etc. It was superceded after independence by *Diário da República* (1975- .).

322 **1980 Angola: special congress report of the Central Committee of the MPLA-Workers Party.**
José Eduardo dos Santos. London: Mozambique, Angola and Guiné Information Centre (MAGIC), 1982. 94p. (MAGIC State Papers and Party Proceedings, Series 3, no. 2).

Report of the MPLA's activities in the period 1978-80 made to the Special Congress of the Party in 1980 by the successor to Agostinho Neto. The report includes an outline of the structure and role of the Party, and other political organizations, as well as a commentary on the socio-economic, political and military situation, and policies to be pursued by the MPLA-PT.

323 **People's Republic of Angola.**
Michael Wolfers. In: *Marxist governments of the world: a world survey. Volume 1: Albania – The Congo.* Edited by Bogdan Szajowski. London: Macmillan, 1981, p. 62-86.

After a brief introduction to the country, this chapter discusses the birth of Angolan nationalism, the period of armed struggle, and the achievement of independence. It then describes the structure of the MPLA and the post-independence government, focusing on major internal and external policies. There is also a short biography of Agostinho Neto and two other members of the MPLA Central Committee.

**Angola: politics, economics and society.**
*See* item no. 263.

**Political development in Afro-Marxist régimes: an analysis of Angola and Mozambique.**
*See* item no. 277.

# Foreign Relations and Foreign Intervention

## General

**324  Angola and the superpowers.**

Edited by K. K. Virmani.   Delhi: Department of African Studies, University of India, 1989. 122p. maps. bibliog.

This book is in two sections. The first, by Mukul Ahmed, examines superpower involvement at the time of Angola's independence. It argues that whilst Soviet policy was consistent, and based on its duty to oppose imperialist aggression, the actions of the US were miscalculated, representing only a desire to restore 'American credibility' after the Vietnam war. The second section, by Poonam Gupta, considers in detail the role of the Soviet Union and China in Angola, both before and after independence. It argues that although Cuban intervention was crucial in securing the MPLA in power, the new Angolan government was still free to develop its own brand of socialism.

**325  Conflict and intervention in Africa: Nigeria, Angola, Zaïre.**

Herbert Ekwe-Ekwe.   London: Macmillan, 1990. 195p. bibliog.

After a general introduction to conflict and external intervention in Africa, chapter 3 of this book analyses the nature of involvement of the United States, the Soviet Union, Cuba, South Africa, and other African states in the internal affairs of Angola since 1975. Five principal themes are explored both for Angola specifically, and in the final two chapters, in comparative perspective for the three countries of the title. These are: the underlying causes of intervention; the type of intervention acceptable to local power groups; the motive for intervention; the form of intervention; and finally any consequences resulting from this action.

326 **Dynamics of Angolan foreign policy.**
Vijay Gupta. *Africa Quarterly* (New Delhi), vol. 28, nos. 1/2 (Jan.-April 1988), p. 8-34.

Discusses the background to Angolan foreign policy in terms of the historical development of the independence movements, as well as the questions of foreign intervention and Angola's own economic interests. The article then proceeds to consider in turn the development of foreign relations with the Eastern Bloc countries, Cuba, the West, Portugal, Zaïre, and South Africa. It argues that foreign policy has been largely externally, rather than internally, driven.

327 **Foreign military intervention in Africa.**
Keith Somerville. London: Pinter; New York: St Martins, 1990. 205p. maps. bibliog.

Provides a general discussion of the causes and consequences of foreign intervention in Africa, spanning the colonial and post-colonial era. At various points, developments in Angola are addressed specifically. Also useful is a general chapter examining the motives behind the United States, Soviet, and Cuban interventions in southern Africa.

328 **Politics in modern Africa: the uneven tribal dimension.**
Kenneth Ingham. London, New York: Routledge, 1990. 248p. bibliog.

A chapter on Angola (p. 176-200) provides a general discussion of political developments through the liberation struggle and independence up to the New York peace accord of 1988. The chapter focuses on the role of external powers.

**Afro-marxist régimes: ideology and public policy.**
*See* item no. 256.

**After Angola: the war over southern Africa.**
*See* item no. 257.

**The 1988 peace accords and the future of south western Africa.**
*See* item no. 274.

# South Africa

329 **Adeus Angola.**
Willem Steenkamp. Cape Town: Howard Timmins, 1976. 145p. maps.

A narrative of the Angolan operations of South African troops in 1975-76, which takes the forms of dispatches written by a journalist at or near the front line. Two concluding essays outline the structure of the South African army, and ask the question, 'was it all worth it?'. The author comments that, at the very least, exposure to full-scale operational conditions provided a much-needed 'shaking up' for the army itself.

330   **African nemesis: war and revolution in southern Africa (1945-2010).**
      Paul L. Moorcraft.   London: Brassey's (UK), 1990. 519p. maps.
      bibliog.
In a book which focuses on the changing military role of South Africa in the region,
two chapters focus specifically on South African connections with Angola, during the
liberation struggle (1961-76) and in the subsequent period of destabilisation (1976-89).
In addition to analysis of the context and causes of this involvement, the book also
provides detailed information on military developments.

331   **Aggression by the apartheid regime against Angola.**
      Holland Committee on Southern Africa (KZA), International
      Commission of Enquiry into the Crimes of the Racist and Apartheid
      Régime in Southern Africa.   Amsterdam: the authors [n.d.]. [36p.]
Published in collaboration with the United Nations Special Committee against
Apartheid, this is a mainly photographic documentation of the process of destabiliza-
tion by the South African government in Angola.

332   **Apartheid's war against Angola.**
      Marga Holness.   New York: United Nations Centre Against
      Apartheid, 1983. 24p. bibliog.
A pamphlet describing the impact of South African aggression in Angola, presenting
estimates of the economic cost of the war damage, and outlining debate in the United
Nations over its reaction to the war.

333   **Borderstrike! South Africa into Angola.**
      Willem Steenkamp.   Durban, South Africa; London: Butterworth,
      1983. 266p.
A detailed eyewitness account of two South African army attacks on 'insurgents' of
SWAPO inside Angola territory, codenamed 'Operation Reindeer' (1978) and
'Operation Sceptic' (1980), as well as a 'follow-up' operation in Zambia. The book
includes numerous photographs of the South African troops, as well as diagrams
showing the logistics of how each battle was won.

334   **The Cuito Cuanavale syndrome: revealing SADF vulnerability.**
      Thomas Ohlson.   *South African Review*, vol. 5 (1989), p. 181-90.
Provides an outline of the key events of the war for southern Angola in 1987/88,
including the defeat of the South African Defence Force (SADF) at Cuito Cuanavale.
The implications of this defeat for the balance of power in the region are also
considered. The impact on southern Africa as a whole is disucussed in a previous
article in the same issue of *South African Review* by Robert Davies.

335 **Documentário fotográfico sobre os crimes da racista Africa do Sul e dos seus lacaios contra a República Popular de Angola.** (Photographic documentary of the crimes of racist South Africa and its lackeys against the People's Republic of Angola.)
República Popular de Angola.  Luanda: Imprensa Nacional, [1983]. [n.p.].

Contains an introduction in Portuguese, French and English, followed by black-and-white photographs, arranged chronologically, from 1975-83. These show the results of South African aggression in various parts of the country on civilians and infrastructural targets. This collection is held by the Centro de Informação e Difusão Amílcar Cabral, along with another, shorter, photographic collection entitled: *Aggression: what the enemies of the people are doing against the People's Republic of Angola*, which was also published in 1983.

336 **Hidden lives, hidden deaths: South Africa's crippling of a continent.**
Victoria Brittain.  London; Boston, Massachusetts: Faber & Faber, 1988. 208p. maps.

A journalistic account of South Africa's attempt to destabilize progressive governments in Black Africa, and the role of the US and the West in supporting them. The book is a readable introduction to the subject, and not surprisingly, contains many references to Angola, including first-hand accounts. Chapter 2, for example, describes the tense situation in southern Angola soon after independence, whilst Chapter 6 focuses on the effect of South African aggression on Huambo district. Brittain is Third World correspondent of the *Guardian* newspaper in the UK.

337 **Stop the war against Angola and Mozambique: chronological account of acts of aggression against the front line states by apartheid South Africa, 1975-1981.**
Jan Marsh.  London: Campaign to Stop the War against Angola and Mozambique (SWAM), 1981. 48p. map.

Details South African military operations in Angola, Mozambique, Zambia and Botswana. The section on Angola covers the 1975-76 invasion, further attacks up to 1979, and the intensified aggression of 1980-81. For each period, the date, place and nature of each attack is tabulated, along with the number of casualties. There is also extended discussion of the politics of destabilization.

**Peacemaking in southern Africa: the Luanda-Pretoria tug of war.**
*See* item no. 275.

**War in Angola: the final South African phase.**
*See* item no. 282.

# Socialist countries

338    **Angola and the Soviet Union since 1975.**
Olayiwola Abegunrin.    *Journal of African Studies*, vol. 14
(spring 1987), p. 25-30.

Examines the foreign policy objectives of independent Angola, and the way in which these have related to military and economic goals. The author argues that although massive military and defence ties were established with the Soviet Union, such close links did not extend to all sectors. In particular, there have been significant economic and trade ties with western countries, which dictated the country's abandonment of Marxism-Leninism, and ensured that the MPLA upheld the principle of free markets.

339    **The Angolan war: a study in Soviet policy in the Third World.**
Arthur J. Klinghoffer.    Boulder, Colorado: Westview, 1980. 229p.
maps. bibliog. (Westview Special Studies on Africa).

Discusses the Soviet and Cuban roles in Angola in the immediate post-independence period, and argues that the war marked a decisive change in Soviet policy, as success led to a considerable increase in their involvement in the Third World in general. However, it is argued that this changing policy represented a reaction to events and the behaviour of the US and other actors, rather than a pre-determined course of action.

340    **The arc of socialist revolutions: Angola to Afghanistan.**
Suzanne Jolicoeur Katsikas.    Cambridge, Massachussetts: Schenkman,
1982. 332p. maps. bibliog.

After an initial chapter which considers the role of the US in the socialist Third World, chapter 2 (p. 55-116) is concerned with Angola. This chapter provides a general introduction to the war in Angola, and to the MPLA and UNITA, which stresses that both the conflict, and the growth of a socialist state, represented responses to local factors, rather than simply being part of a Soviet grand design for international communism. Individual sections then focus on the Cuban intervention, US interests, and continuing political and economic problems.

341    **Changing the history of Africa: Angola and Namibia.**
Edited by David Deutschmann.    Melbourne, Australia: Ocean Press,
1989. 153p. maps.

A collections of writings presenting a Cuban perspective on that country's involvement in Angola since independence. It includes an interview with Jorge Risque, head of the Foreign Relations Department of the Communist Party of Cuba; speeches by Fidel Castro and the Cuban Defence Minister, Raúl Castro; texts of accords signed at the United Nations; and articles by Columbian novelist Gabriel García Marquéz, and Cuban journalist Félix Pita Astudillo, on Cuba's role. Also included are a number of photographs documenting the Cuban presence in Angola.

342  **Cuba in Africa.**
Edited by Carmelo Mesa-Lago, June S. Belkin.   Pittsburg,
Pennsylvania: University of Pittsburg, Centre for Latin American
Studies, 1982. 230p. bibliog. (Latin American Monograph and
Document Series, no. 3).

Includes four major essays, on Cuban-Soviet relations, Cuban involvement in the Horn
of Africa, political/military and finally economic aspects of Cuban involvement in
Africa, each supported by two commentaries. Most authors are political scientists
residing in Cuba. As a whole, the book plays down the significance of Cuban
involvement, and in the case of Angola, suggests that it was South African support for
UNITA, rather than Soviet support for the MPLA, which exerted a controlling
influence on the continued presence of Cuban troops. With the exception of part 2
which covers the Horn of Africa, the Angolan situation is discussed in its own right
throughout the book. Also included is a useful bibliography specifically on Cuban
relations with Angola.

343  **Les cubains et l'Afrique: avec les interviews de M. M. Mohamed
Warsame, Gerhard Chaliaud, Eduardo Manet, du general Buis et du
chercheur belge.** (The Cubans and Africa: including interviews with
Mohamed Warsame, Gerhard Chaliaud, Eduardo Manet, General
Buis, and a Belgian researcher.)
Ezzedine Mestiri.   Paris: Karthala, 1980. 239p. maps. bibliog.

A hostile account of Cuban involvement in Africa, based on press reports and
interviews with the Somali ambassador to France, a Cuban dissident, and other
'experts' on African politics. The book concludes that Cuban involvement in Angola,
as elsewhere in Africa, was a response to direct orders from Moscow.

344  **The demise of the world revolutionary process: Soviet-Angolan relations
under Gorbachev.**
Michael McFaul.   *Journal of Southern African Studies*, vol. 16, no. 1
(March 1990), p. 165-89.

A discussion of Soviet-Angolan relations initially from a Soviet perspective, which
examines changing thinking in Moscow about 'regional security' in the Gorbachev era.
The implications of these changes for Angola are then considered. It is suggested that
in economic terms, the effect has been minimal, since economic ties were never strong
between the two countries, and restructuring of the Angolan economy on market lines
had already begun. Much more important was the effect of changing Soviet attitudes
on Angola's own regional policy, as pressure was placed on the government to
negotiate with UNITA, and participate in the US-brokered peace settlement for
Namibia.

345  **Disengagement from southwest Africa: the prospects for peace in Angola
and Namibia.**
Edited by Owen Ellison Kahn.   New Brunswick, New Jersey:
Transaction, 1991. 244p. maps. (East-South Relations Series).

Consists of papers from a conference of political scientists in 1988 on the Soviet role in
Angola and Namibia. After a general introduction, and a brief profile of Angola by the
editor, this book is divided into four main sections, dealing in turn with Soviet, Cuban

and South African interventions in the region, and the position of Angola and Namibia in East-West relations. The focus in all chapters is on the Angola-Namibia accords of 1988, and the realignments of foreign policy that preceeded them. An appendix addresses the dialogue between UNITA and the Soviet Union, including a presentation by Marcos Samondo, a member of the UNITA Central Committee.

346 **Moscow, Havana and the MPLA takeover of Angola.**
Gerhardus S. Labuschagne.   Pretoria: Foreign Affairs Association, 1976. 8p. (Foreign Affairs Association, Study Report no. 3).
An account by a South African academic of Soviet and Cuban interests in Angola, which argues that the use of Cuban troops provided the Soviet Union with an important new weapon to spread communism and influence the conduct of liberation movements.

347 **Operation Carlota.**
C. García Márquez, translated from the Spanish by Patrick Camiller.
*New Left Review*, vol. 101/2 (Feb.-April 1977), p. 123-37.
An account of the successful intervention of Cuban troops in Angola in support of MPLA forces after independence. The author argues that this was carried out through a spirit of internationalism, and was crucial in ensuring an MPLA victory over the Zaïrean and South African armies.

348 **Southern Africa since the Portuguese coup.**
Edited by John Seiler.   Boulder, Colorado: Westview, 1980. 252p. (Westview Special Studies on Africa).
This edited volume includes two chapters on the Cuban and Soviet roles in Angola. The former, by Maurice Halperin, accepts that the Soviet Union was a prime mover in determining Cuban foreign policy, but draws attention also to the long history of Cuban involvement in Africa, and the particular agendas thrown up by the Cuban revolution and its leader, Fidel Castro. The latter, by Christopher Stevens, argues that Soviet involvement after independence aimed for diplomatic and political gains, rather than immediate military or strategic advantage. The book also includes an introductory chapter by Douglas Wheeler on Portuguese withdrawal, which focuses on the Angolan case.

349 **Soviet strategy in southern Africa: Gorbachev's pragmatic approach.**
Peter Vanneman.   Stanford, California: Hoover Institution Press, 1990. 142p. bibliog.
Chapter 5 of this work, which deals with Angola (p. 45-57) documents what the author describes as three decades of Soviet involvement in Angola. It argues that the recent escalation of intervention, especially in 1987/88, signalled the Soviet Union's continuing commitment to support the Angolan marxist régime, and justified the renewal of US financial support for UNITA. A book quickly outpaced by events.

# Western countries

350 **Angola, Mozambique and the West.**
Edited by H. Kitchen. New York, London: Praeger, 1987. 154p.
(The Washington Papers, no. 130).

Includes five chapters on Angola. The first three, written by John Marcum in 1983, 1984 and 1985 respectively, examine the social and political background of UNITA; the conduct of the war between UNITA and government forces; and the options for United States involvement in the struggle. He argues for a stance of patient diplomacy, rather than military intervention. Two further chapters by Gillian Gunn, written in 1986 and 1987 respectively, survey the Angolan economy, and provide a summary of Cuban involvement in the country.

351 **Angola: the hidden history of Washington's war.**
Ernest Harsch, Tony Thomas, with an introduction by Malik Miah.
New York: Pathfinder, 1976. 159p.

Written by a journalist and a leader of the Socialist Workers Party, this book examines the strategic interest of Angola to the United States, Portugal and South Africa, as well as some of the divisions in the nationalist camp after independence. It calls for an end to US and other foreign interventions in the country.

352 **Brazil and Africa.**
José Honório Rodrigues, translated from the Portuguese by Richard A.
Mazzara. Los Angeles, California; Berkeley, California: University of California Press, 1965. 382p.

Part 1 of this book reviews Anglo-Brazilian relations from 1500-1960, whilst part 2 draws specific policy conclusions for the conduct of Brazilian foreign relations. The book argues that from the 17th to 19th centuries, Brazil maintained stronger ties with Angola than did Portugal itself, and that at the time of Brazilian independence, two of Angola's three deputies to the Portuguese Cortes cast their lot with Brazil. It also argues that Brazil, to be consistent to its anti-colonialism, should support the Angolan struggle for independence.

353 **The cold war guerilla: Jonas Savimbi, the US media, and the Angolan war.**
Elaine Windrich. New York: Greenwood, 1992. 183p. bibliog.
(Contributions to the Study of Mass Media and Communications, no. 31).

Analyses material printed in the United States mainstream press on Angola, and Jonas Savimbi's UNITA in particular. It argues that a sophisiticated and sanitized image of Savimbi as a freedom fighter has been portrayed in the US media as a result of information supplied and pressure from the Reagan and Bush administrations. Similarly, US foreign policy in the region has been labelled a success on the basis of selective reporting, which has ignored or challenged evidence of human rights abuses by UNITA.

354   **Globalism or regionalism? United States policy towards southern Africa.**
Garrick Uttley.   London: International Institute for Strategic Studies,
1979. 36p. (Adelphi Papers, no. 154).
A review of US policy and interests in four southern African countries: South Africa,
Rhodesia, Namibia and Angola. Of historical interest, the chapter on Angola (p. 23-
32) is a largely factual account of changes in US policy from 1975-78, whilst a final
chapter draws out general themes in all four countries.

355   **In search of enemies: a CIA story.**
John Stockwell.   London: Futura, 1979. rev. ed. 304p. maps.
A stinging indictment of the United States Central Intelligence Agency's operations in
Angola after the revolution, written by the former chief of the CIA's Angolan Task
Force in the crucial period of 1975-76. Includes chapters on Jonas Savimbi and Holden
Roberto, the hiring of foreign mercenaries and other illegal methods employed by the
CIA team, as well as an analysis of why the US-backed forces failed.

356   **Memorandum on the Clark Amendment: the US threat to destabilize
Angola.**
Marga Holness.   London: Mozambique, Angola and Guiné
Information Centre (MAGIC), 1981. 5p.
A short note which draws attention to America's 'undeclared war' on the Angolan
people, and argues for the upholding by the Reagan administration of the Clark
Amendment, which banned US military aid to UNITA and the FNLA in 1976.

357   **Operação Africa: a conspiração antiafricana em Portugal.** (Operation
Africa: the anti-African conspiracy in Portugal.)
Fernando Semedo, João Paulo Guerra.   Lisbon: Caminho, 1984. 105p.
A short, but detailed account by two Portuguese journalists which examines relations
between right-wing groups in Portugal, the CIA, the South African secret service,
BOSS, and UNITA.

358   **Regional conflict and US policy: Angola and Mozambique.**
Edited by Richard J. Bloomfield.   Algonac, Michigan: Reference
Publications, 1988. 261p. map. bibliog.
Includes eight essays by prominent historians and political scientists. Two deal
specifically with Angola, covering the role of the Cuban armed forces, and United
States foreign policy respectively. The latter contribution, by Gerald Bender, criticizes
America's tough stance, arguing that the economic reforms already implemented are
worthy of US encouragement. All except one of the remaining essays deal with the
region as a whole, analysing the legacy of Portuguese colonial rule and the
decolonization process; South Africa's regional hegemony; the role of the Soviet
Union, with a concluding chapter by the editor that assesses US strategic interests.

## 359  Secret weapon in Africa.
Oleg Ignatiev, translated from the Russian by David Fidlon.  Moscow: Progress, 1977. 188p.

This short study explores the foreign interventions in Angola both during the anti-colonial struggle, and in the immediate post-independence period. In the introduction, the background to US, UN and Soviet interests in the region are outlined. Subsequent chapters then establish the connections of Holden Roberto (of the FNLA) and Jonas Savimbi (of UNITA) with the CIA and the Portuguese secret police (PIDE), as well as with China, and South Africa. The activities of foreign mercenaries in the country in the immediate post-independence conflict are also considered.

## 360  Trilateral aid: Portugal's aid relationship with its former African colonies.
Shirley Washington.  In: *Culture and development in Africa*. Edited by Stephen H. Arnold, Andre Nitecki.  Trenton, New Jersey: Africa World Press, 1990, p. 187-96.

Although there is nothing in this article that specifically refers to Angola, it does explain the main patterns of Portugal's relationship with all its former colonies since 1975. Also included is a useful introduction to Portuguese institutions concerned with Africa.

## 361  US policy towards Angola since 1975.
Inge Tvedten.  *Journal of Modern African Studies*, vol. 30, no. 1 (March 1992), p. 31-52.

Argues that after the 1988 New York accord, United States policy towards Angola, involving continued support for UNITA, and blocking of the country's full membership of the IMF and World Bank, has significantly delayed the finding of a lasting solution to the Angolan conflict. The article includes a discussion of the peace process itself, and of social and economic conditions in Angola, as well as exploring and questioning the motivations behind US policy.

## 362  US policy towards Angola: the Kissinger years, 1974-76.
George Wright.  Leeds, England: African Studies Unit, University of Leeds, 1990. 23p. (Leeds Southern African Studies, no. 2).

Examines the basis for United States political involvement in Angola during the early post-independence period. The author identifies a struggle between the 'globalist', and inherently interventionist stance of Kissinger and the White House, and contrasts this with the 'regionalist' stance of Congress, which eventually prevailed, albeit only for a few years.

# Economic Development

## General

363 **Angola: an introductory economic review.**
Washington, DC: World Bank, 1991.
A comprehensive account of the Angolan economy, based on a UNDP-funded mission to Angola by various consultants in late 1987. Three principal difficulties for the economy are identified: the continuing war, which has destroyed a substantial part of social and economic infrastructure, made much of the countryside unsafe, and required high military spending; unusually severe human resource constraints, resulting from the loss of skilled workers after Portuguese withdrawal; and inadequate economic policies. Concerning the latter difficulty, there is a review of the Economic and Financial Restructuring (SEF) package which was adopted in 1987, and recommendations to control domestic demand, stimulate domestic supply (through the establishment of incentives for the private sector), and improve allocation of public expenditure. Also included are many statistical tables on all aspects of the Angolan economy.

364 **Economia de Angola.** (The economy of Angola.)
Fátima Roque, Pedro Pita Barros, Ana Maria Neto, Rui Sousa
Monteiro, Vitorino Domingos Hussi, Pedro Santa Clara Gomes, João
Miguel Ejarque. Lisbon: Bertrand Editora, 1991. 335p. bibliog.
A recent study of the Angolan economy, which provides a useful introduction to the failures of both the colonial system, and the planned socialist economy after independence. It starts with a review of the development of the colonial economy during the course of the 20th century, including a statistical summary of its major characteristics at the time of independence. Three cycles of economic growth are identified, linked to the slave trade, the coffee boom, and more recently, the sale of petroleum. Then, government macro-economic policy in the post-independence period is considered, including the development of budget deficits, commerial, monetary and exchange policy, and interventions in the fields of prices and incomes, investment,

agriculture, industry, mineral resources, and transport. Two final chapters focus in detail on the Economic and Financial Restructuring (SEF) programme of 1987, and co-operation between Angola and Portugal, the SADCC (Southern African Development Co-ordination Conference), the European Community, and foreign investors in general.

365 **Macroeconomic studies: Angola.**
Renato Aguilar, Mário Zejan. Stockholm: Swedish International Development Authority, Planning Secretariat, 1990. 59p. bibliog. (SIDA Macroeconomic Studies, no. 12/90).
Analyses the background to the current economic problems of Angola, and examines the potential solutions, focusing in particular on fiscal and monetary policy, and external debt. Information is reviewed on the colonial economy, population and trends in GDP, as well as current production in each of the main sectors of the economy. Changes in prices, wages, and the exchange rate are then analysed, along with fiscal policy and foreign trade. Two final sections then focus in detail on the Economic and Financial Restructuring (SEF) programme introduced in 1987, as well as the alternatives for future economic policy.

**Poverty and food insecurity in Luanda.**
*See* item no. 231.

**The agro-based industries in Angola: key characteristics and rehabilitation issues.**
*See* item no. 395.

# Colonial economy

366 **Actividade Económica de Angola: Revista de Estudos Económicos.**
(Economic Activity of Angola: Journal of Economic Studies.)
Luanda: Direcção Provincial dos Serviços de Economia, 1935-74.
tri-annual.
This colonial economic journal contained a wide variety of articles and reports, many relating to government plans or activities in the economic sphere.

367 **Angola on the road to progress.**
Michael Chapman. Luanda: Angola Consultantes, 1971. 94p. maps.
An introduction to Angola, covering territory and government, education, labour and welfare policies, natural resources, industry, tourism, foreign investment and trade. Extensive statistical tables are included, as are lists of major indigenous and foreign companies, economic institutions, and trade representatives. The book, which is in English and Portuguese, aims to encourage overseas investment in the colonial economy.

368   **Angola: Economic and Financial Survey.**
Lisbon: Banco de Angola, Economic Studies Department, 1960-73.
annual.
This useful survey from the late colonial era includes information on agriculture, fisheries, mining, manufacturing, construction, electricity, transport, external trade, and public finance, as well as the activities of the Banco de Angola. It also includes numerous tables and graphs.

369   **Angola: estrutura económica e classes sociais.** (Angola: economic structure and social classes.)
Henrique Guerra.   Lisbon: Edições 70, 1979. 4th ed. 168p. maps.
bibliog. (Estudos: Autores Angolanos, no. 2).
An important introductory summary of the colonial economy and society of Angola, from a Marxist perspective, written in a Portuguese jail by the author in 1972/73 and first published in 1975. In part 1, it outlines the structure and linkages of Portuguese capital and the international imperialist system, with a number of profiles of major Portuguese companies; also included is information about the colonial state, and African producers. In part 2, there is a description of the major class fractions of Angolan society. A final section of notes provides further information about Portuguese companies, and some statistical material.

370   **Commerce, industry and empire: the making of modern Portuguese colonialism in Angola and Mozambique, 1890-1914.**
Gregory Roger Pirio.   PhD thesis, University of California, Los Angeles, 1982. (Available from University Microfilms, Ann Arbor, Michigan, order no. 8225600).
An exploration of the evolution of the Portuguese colonial economy at the turn of the 20th century, which concentrates on Mozambique, but includes numerous references to Angola as well.

371   **How to invest in Angola.**
Walter Marques, translated from the Portuguese by F. Hollis.
Luanda: Junta de Desenvolvimento Industrial, Fundo de Fomento de Produção e Exportação, 1963. 42p. maps. bibliog.
Although obviously dated, this pamphlet does include some useful information and maps of climatic zones and natural resources, as well as providing material of historical interest on transport infrastructures, economic activities, power generation, and colonial development plans and investment legislation.

372   **Imperial network and external dependency: the case of Angola.**
William Minter.   Beverley Hills, California: Sage, 1972. 70p. bibliog.
(Sage Professional Papers: International Studies Series, no. 1).
Based on the author's MA thesis at the University of Wisconsin, this short book analyses the Angolan economy from the perspective of the 'dependency' school of development studies. The level of economic development, through trade, direct investment, finance and technology, as well as political and cultural dependence in the colony is assessed. The evolution of colonial and neo-colonial dependency networks is

also analysed, and these are illustrated diagrammatically. There are various useful statistical tables.

373 **L'enjeu economique international d'une décolonisation: le cas de l'Angola.** (The international stake in decolonization: the case of Angola.)
Centre de Recherche et d'Information Socio-Politique (CRISP). Brussels: CRISP, 1975. 2 vols. (Courrier Hebdomadaire, nos 671-72).

Two short reports on the political and economic situation in Angola as it was immediately after independence, placed in its international context. Volume 1 discusses the the structure of Angola's economy, presenting available statistics from the colonial era. Then, volume 2 looks in detail at foreign interests in the country, focusing separately on Portuguese, Belgian, United States, United Kingdom and South African companies. It argues that the Angolan economy is characterized by dependency, which needed to be broken in order to achieve social justice and development.

374 **Portuguese colonialism from South Africa to Europe.**
Eduardo de Sousa Ferreira. Freiburg, Germany: Aktion Dritte Welt, 1972. 232p. maps. bibliog. (Economic and Political Studies on the Portuguese Colonies, South Africa, and Namibia).

An analysis of the colonial economy of the Portuguese territories in Africa, written in the last days of Portuguese imperialism, by an exiled Portuguese economist. This work attacks Portuguese colonial rule, as well as the support offered to it by European nations, the United States, and South Africa.

375 **Portuguese West Africa: economic and social conditions in Portuguese West Africa (Angola).**
D. O. Fynes-Clinton. London: HMSO, 1949. 39p. (Overseas Economic Surveys).

A description of the economy of Angola, covering finance, production, natural resources, trade, legislation and transport, with numerous statistical tables.

376 **Revolution in Angola.**
Members of the Liberation Front [MPLA]. London: Merlin Press, 1972. 62p.

An economic background to the liberation struggle written under the auspices of the MPLA in London. Includes a useful outline of the colonial economy and society, and the MPLA's strategy for economic development after independence. Also covered are the international links of the colonial economy.

**Industrialização de Angola: reflexão sobre a experiência da administração portuguesa, 1961-1975.** (Industrialization of Angola: reflections on the experience of the Portuguese administration, 1961-1975.)
*See* item no. 399.

**Communications and hydraulic developments in Guinea, Angola and Moçambique.**
*See* item no. 418.

**Bibliografia sobre a Economia Portuguesa.** (Bibliography on the Portuguese Economy.)
*See* item no. 556.

# Post-independence economy

377   **Africa Económica.** (Economic Africa.)
      Lisbon: Centro de Estudos Economia e Sociedade, 1985- . quarterly.
Provides a digest of information from various periodical publications on Lusophone Africa, aimed at the business community. Each issue includes a separate section on the Angolan economy.

378   **Angola 1991: a long and hard way to the marketplace.**
      Renato Aguilar, Mario Zejan.   Stockholm: Swedish International Development Authority (SIDA), 1991. 47p. (SIDA Macroeconomic Studies, no. 19/91).
Second of two reports by the authors on the Angolan economy (q.v.), which examines recent economic performance by sector, as well as the economic reforms of September 1990 (*Programa de Acção do Governo*), and their social and economic consequences.

379   **Angola's political economy, 1975-1985.**
      M. R. Bhagavan.   Uppsala, Sweden: Scandinavian Institute of African Studies, 1986. 89p. (Scandinavian Institute of African Studies, Research Report, no. 75).
A survey of the political economy of Angola, which deals with the economic and political background to independence, and then analyses the continuing crisis caused by the war and the collapse of industry. In conclusion, the conditions required for socialist development are outlined. Numerous statistical tables are included, whilst a postscript provides details of war damage to the economy.

380   **Angola, São Tomé e Príncipe: Country Profile.**
      London: Economist Intelligence Unit, 1989- . annual.
An authoritative annual review aimed at the business community, covering political background, population and society, followed by a fairly detailed description of the economy, including trends in the previous year. Separate sections are devoted to each of the major economic sectors (agriculture, manufacturing, mining, etc.).

381 **Angola, São Tomé e Príncipe: Country Report.**
London: Economist Intelligence Unit, 1989- . quarterly.
Each issue contains statistical information on the country and its economy, followed by a brief 'outlook', and a wide-ranging review of political and economic developments during the quarter.

382 **Angolan Business.**
Luanda: People's Republic of Angola, 1990- . quarterly.
A new English-language magazine covering aspects of the Angolan economy, and changes in rules for foreign investors. The first issue included a number of useful addresses of Angolan organizations and companies.

383 **Confiscos e nacionalizações na República Popular de Angola.**
(Confiscations and nationalizations in the People's Republic of Angola.)
Luanda: Departamento de Educação Política e Ideológica, 1978. 46p.
A list of businesses which were nationalized, or whose assets were confiscated after independence. The list is organized by economic sector.

384 **Economic policy in Angola: strategy of development and economic system regulation.**
Mário Murteira. Lisbon: Centro de Estudos Economia e Sociedade, 1983. 15p.
Examines some of the economic adjustment policies forced on the Angolan government after eight years of civil war, and makes further recommendations for changes. In particular, the author argues that priority should be given to the development of peasant agriculture, and less emphasis placed on prestige industrial projects. The report includes tables of estimated GDP and external trade. It is held at the Centro de Informação e Difusão Amílcar Cabral in Box No. A-PE II.5. The same box also contains an unpublished version of the 1991 economic plan, as well as some earlier economic plans, such as that of the Provisional Government of 1975.

385 **Establishing the conditions for socialism: the case of Angola.**
M. R. Bhagavan. In: *Africa: problems in the transition to socialism.*
Edited by Barry Munslow. London, New Jersey: Zed Press, 1986, p. 140-51.
This chapter provides an accessible background to the attempt to build a socialist economy in Angola. First, the state of the country's political economy prior to independence is considered. Then, attention is turned to economic problems after independence resulting from external aggression, and the extent of revolutionary transformation of the economy. A postscript describes the economic situation in 1984/85. Also included are numerous statistical tables, including estimates of war damage to the economy.

386 **People's Republic of Angola: economic summary.**
Luanda: Ministry of Finance, 1989. 17p.

A useful introduction to the economy of Angola, including basic statistical data, and notes on its history, and structure. The oil, agriculture, coffee, fisheries, diamonds and manufacturing sectors are briefly discussed, as are public finance, inflation, the balance of payments and international debt. The Economic and Financial Restructuring (SEF) programme, and other recent economic policy adjustments are also outlined.

387 **Pouvoir populaire et cooperatives en Angola (1974-1977): cooperatives de consommation a Luanda et cooperatives de production a Malange.**
(Popular power and co-operatives in Angola [1974-1977]: consumer co-operatives in Luanda and production co-operatives in Malanje.)
Valdir Carlos Sarapu. Paris: Ecole des Hautes Etudes en Sciences Sociales, 1980. 242p. bibliog.

Based on his diploma thesis in social science, this study examines the rise of '*poder popular*', or popular power in Angola after independence, and its influence on the co-operative sector. In the first part, popular power is defined, and its history traced from its emergence to later institutionalisation. Parts 2 and 3 then focus on case studies of co-operatives in the consumer sector in Luanda, and in agricultural production in Malange district. The organization, political significance, and ultimate marginalization of these co-operatives is traced, as they were forced to adjust to the centralization desired by the MPLA government.

388 **Prospects and problems of the transition from agrarianism to socialism: the case of Angola, Guinea-Bissau and Mozambique.**
Tetteh A. Kofi. *World Development*, vol. 9, no. 9/10 (Sept.-Oct. 1981), p. 851-70.

Analyses the attempt in each country to forge a socialist development path based on popular power (*poder popular*). The article starts by considering the theoretical basis for socialist development, and then examines the colonial political economy in each country. Finally, it assesses some of the initial and more fundamental problems faced as socialist transformation was attempted.

389 **The second economy in Angola: *esquema* and *candonga*.**
Daniel dos Santos. In: *The second economy in marxist states*. Edited by Maria Los. London: Macmillan, 1990, p. 157-74.

A description of the second or informal economy in Angola, which discusses the circulation of goods and services beyond the centrally-planned sector, in both illegal and legal activities. The article argues that the second economy is not subordinate to the official economy, but rather that each is mutually reinforcing.

**Angola: socialism at birth.**
*See* item no. 129.

**Economic Development.** Post-independence economy

**Afro-marxist régimes: ideology and public policy.**
*See* item no. 256.

**Angola: politics, economics and society.**
*See* item no. 263.

**Angola: prospects for socialist industrialization.**
*See* item no. 397.

# Trade and Finance

390   **Câmara de Comércio e Indústria Portugal-Angola.** (Portugal-Angola
      Chamber of Commerce and Industry.)
      Lisbon: Cámara de Comércio e Indústria Portugal-Angola, 1988- .
      bi-monthly.
A magazine devoted to business links between Portugal and Angola.

391   **Comércio Externo. Publicação económica angolana.** (External Trade.
      Angolan economic publication.)
      Luanda: República Popular de Angola, 1986- . monthly.
A monthly trade magazine produced by the Angolan government.

392   **Ecos e Certames: FILDA 87 suplemento.** (Echoes and contests: FILDA
      87 supplement.)
      Luanda: Ecos e Certames, 1987. Special Issue.
A special issue of the Luanda-based trade magazine produced for the 4th International
Fair of Luanda (FILDA) in 1987, which contains a number of articles about commerce
and external trade, as well as development funds available from the European
Community. The journal is available at the Centro de Informação e Difusão Amílcar
Cabral, in Lisbon (Box No. AO-Com I.11). In the same box file are government
documents on external trade produced for the previous international fair.

393   **The effects of Portugal's accession to the European Community on the
      exports of the ACP countries.**
      Matthew McQueen, Robert Read.   *Estudos de Economia*, vol. 6,
      no. 3 (April-June 1986), p. 369-84.
Questions the assumption that ACP exports would complement those of existing
European nations at the time of the third enlargement of the European Community in
1986. Specifically, the authors argue that for a range of products, Portugal and the

ACP states, including Angola, would compete with each other to sell products in the community, leading to increased protectionism against the latter group. The implications for Angola of Portuguese accession are briefly considered.

394  **Investimento estrangeiro em Angola: formulários para apresentação de propostas.** (Foreign investment in Angola: procedure for the presentation of proposals.)
Lisbon, Luanda: Câmara de Comércio e Indústria Portugal-Angola, 1990. [n.p.]. (Cadernos Económicos Portugal-Angola, no. 3).
A short introductory guide to investors in Angola, which reproduces the rather lengthy forms still required to set up business links in the country.

**Angola: an introductory economic review.**
*See* item no. 363.

**Macroeconomic studies: Angola.**
*See* item no. 365.

**Estatística das Contribuições e Impostos.** (Tax and excise statistics.)
*See* item no. 427.

**Estatística do Comércio Externo.** (External trade statistics.)
*See* item no. 429.

# Industry and Industrialization

395   **The agro-based industries in Angola: key characteristics and rehabilitation issues.**
United Nations Industrial Development Organization (UNIDO).
Vienna: UNIDO Regional and Country Studies Branch, Industrial
Policy and Perspectives Division, 1988. 46p. map. bibliog. (Studies in
the Rehabilitation of African Industry, no. 5).

Based on a one-month UNIDO field mission to Angola in 1988, this report presents the results of a survey into the rehabilitation needs of the country's agricultural-related industry. After a very general outline of the Angolan economy, and the manufacturing sector in particular, changes in the food processing sector are highlighted, including an examination of the linkages between plants, and with other sectors of the economy. A very useful section of the report then discusses government policy, and the development plans of companies operating in Angola. Finally, recommendations are made for support for the rehabilitation process from the international community.

396   **Angola: economic reconstruction and rehabilitation.**
Vienna: United Nations Industrial Development Organisation
(UNIDO), 1990. 75p. bibliog. (UNIDO Industrial Development
Review Series).

A review of the industrial situation in Angola as of 1988, and its prospects for rehabilitation. Includes the growth and performance of the manufacturing sector, problems of selected enterprises, the policy and institutional framework for development, and the country's natural and infrastructural resources. Appendices contain statistical tables, laws relating to foreign investment, and a list of UNIDO-sponsored projects.

397 **Angola: prospects for socialist industrialization.**
M. R. Bhagavan. Uppsala, Sweden: Scandinavian Institute of African Affairs, 1980. 48p. (Scandinavian Institute of African Studies, Research Report no. 57).

A short paper which examines in detail the structure of manufacturing production left by the Portuguese in 1975, and the country's position in the international division of labour. On this basis, it addresses in broad terms the strategy of the MPLA to break away from this division of labour, and pursue a policy of socialist industrialization. The success of such a strategy is seen as depending both on the extent of foreign destabilization of the economy, and on the outcome of a continuing internal class struggle.

398 **Industrial development strategy: final report of the coordination group.**
Walter Marques, Alberto Diogo, Teles Grilo, Marques da Mata, Morgado Cândido, translated from the Portuguese by Carmo Vaz, António da Fonseca. Luanda: Secretária Provincial da Economia, Gabinete de Estudos (Provincial Secretariat for Economic Affairs, Centre for Economic Studies), 1971. 153p.

An introduction provides a general outline of the industrial structure of Angola, and a proposed Industrial Development Strategy for the colony. The bulk of the book then deals in detail with factors constraining industrial development, including policy, finance, management and marketing factors; as well as other issues such as the promotion of economic integration, and the maintenance of quality standards. A final section then presents details of the Industrial Development Strategy, with the legal and development implications for different industries. Further details on the economic situation in individual sectors are contained in extensive appendices.

399 **Industrialização de Angola: reflexão sobre a experiência da administração portuguesa, 1961-1975.** (Industrialization of Angola: reflections on the experience of the Portuguese administration, 1961-1975.)
Ana Maria Neto. Lisbon: Escher, 1991. 108p. (Colecção Estudos sobre Africa, no. 3).

One of a spate of recent books in Portuguese taking an in-depth look at the economy of Angola, based on the last decade-and-a-half of colonial rule. It examines the impact of attempts to integrate the province into the metropolitan economy, including the successes and failures of that policy. A number of statistical tables are included, making this a useful source book.

**Estatística Industrial.** (Industrial statistics.)
*See* item no. 431.

# Mining and Natural Resources

400   **A pesca artesanal em Angola: estudo sócio-económica do apoio sueco à pesca artesanal em Angola.** (Craft fisheries in Angola: a socio-economic study of Swedish aid to the craft fisheries in Angola.)
Lasse Krantze, translated from the Swedish by Luís Mexêdo.
Stockholm: University of Stockholm, 1984. 36p.

A report on Swedish aid to the traditional fishing industries in Luanda, Barra do Dande, Ambriz, Soyo and Cabinda. Includes analysis of the problems of co-operatives set up in this sector since independence. This study is available at the Centro de Informação e Difusão Amílcar Cabral in Lisbon (Ref AO-P I.1).

401   **Revista energia.** (Energy review.)
Luanda: Empresa Nacional de Electricidade, 1982- . quarterly.

A magazine about the energy sector in Angola produced by the state electricity company. Its current status is uncertain.

402   **SADCC Energy.**
Luanda: SADCC Energy Sector Technical and Administration Unit, 1983- . quarterly.

Reports on developments in the energy sector of the SADCC countries. Given the importance of oil in Angola, and the fact that SADCC's Energy Sector Technical and Administation Unit is located in Luanda, this magazine regularly included features on Angola. The current status of the periodical is uncertain.

# Agriculture and Rural Development

403 **Agriculture in the Congo basin: tradition and change in African rural economies.**
Marvin P. Miracle. Madison, Wisconsin: University of Wisconsin Press, 1967. 355p. maps. bibliog.

Although ostensibly on the Congo basin, which includes parts of northern Angola, this book focuses almost exclusively on the part of the basin in present day Zaïre. Nonetheless, its English-language description of different agricultural systems and technological change is of some interest to the student of northern Angolan agriculture.

404 **Algumas considerações sobre a agricultura em Angola.** (Some reflections on agriculture in Angola.)
Joao Heitor Mirrado. *Revista de Ciências Agrárias*, vol. 7, no. 2 (July 1989), p. 37-58.

A useful article which describes the history, development and current importance of agriculture in the Angolan economy. Includes a chronological table of significant government projects and interventions in the agricultural sector, as well as a resumé of the role of different government institutes in the post-independence period, and tables of agricultural exports. The same issue of *Revista de Ciências Agrárias* also includes an article by Vasco Antunes Sousa Dias entitled '*Aspectos da pecuária em Angola*' (Aspects of livestock farming in Angola) (p. 59-96), which lists the main breeds of livestock kept in Angola, as well as their major pests, and the significance of industries related to the livestock sector.

405    **Campo. Revista Mensal do Centro de Documentação e Difusão Técnica do Ministério de Agricultura.** (Field. Monthly Review of the Documentation and Technical Dissemination Centre of the Ministry of Agriculture.)
Luanda: República Popular de Angola, 1979-81. monthly.

An agricultural magazine produced by the government aimed at stimulating production. Its fate after 1981 is unknown.

406    **Contribuição para o estudo das características dos cafés de Angola.** (Contribution towards the study of the characteristics of the coffees of Angola.)
A. Baião Esteves, J. Santos Oliveira.    Lisbon: Junta de Investigações do Ultramar, 1970. 177p. map. bibliog. (Estudos, Ensaios e Documentos, no. 126).

An in-depth study of the coffee produced in colonial Angola which starts with a general discussion of coffee and its importance as an export crop. There is then a detailed description of the physical and chemical properties of the coffees of Angola, based on samples taken from a number of zones of production around the country. There is also a section on the technology of coffee production. Numerous statistical tables are also included on this major export crop, once a mainstay of the Angolan economy.

407    **The ecology of malnutrition in seven countries of southern Africa and in Portuguese Guinea: the Republic of South Africa, South West Africa (Namibia), Botswana, Lesotho, Swaziland, Mozambique, Angola, Portuguese Guinea.**
Jacques M. May, Donna L. McLellan.    New York: Hafner, 1971. 432p. maps. bibliog. (Studies in Medical Geography, vol. 10).

A sixty-three page chapter on Angola in this study provides considerable information on the food resources of the country, outlining the means of production (labour, farms, fertilisers, and equipment), food production itself, food industries, trade and food distribution. Also discussed are diets, the adequacy of food resources, and patterns of nutritional disease. There is a useful introduction to the physical and human geography of the country. Although some of the specific information and tabulated data provided are now of historical interest only, there is also much background information on conditions for food production which is relevant to present-day planners.

408    **Flora infestante das culturas de Angola.** (Weeds in Angola.)
J. Brito Teixeira.    Nova Lisboa (Chianga), Angola: IV Jornadas Silvo Agronómicas, 1965. 3p.

A list of the weeds affecting coffee in Amboim, sisal in Ganda, and sugar cane in Benguela and Dandé. Another paper from the same conference deals with the cultivation of bananas (*Contribuição para o fomento da cultura da banana em Angola* [Contribution towards the promotion of banana cultivation in Angola] by Abílio Mendes Gaspar, A. Castanheira Diniz). Both are available at the Centro de Informação e Difusão Amílcar Cabral (Ref. AO-Agr I.19).

409 **The food crisis and the socialist state in Lusophone Africa.**
Rosemary E. Galli. *African Studies Review*, vol. 30, no. 1
(March 1987), p. 19-44.
Discusses attempts at agricultural development both in the colonial era, and since
independence. In particular, attempts to establish Agricultural Development Stations
(EDAs) to mobilise peasant production are considered. The initial failure of this policy
is seen as resulting from continuation of the war.

410 **Gazeta Agrícola.** (Agrarian Gazette.)
Luanda: Edição da Gazeta Agrícola de Angola, 1956-75. monthly.
A publication of the colonial *Associação dos Agricultores de Angola*, which provided
news and information to farmers up to independence.

411 **The growth and decline of African agriculture in central Angola, 1890-
1950.**
Linda Heywood. *Journal of Southern African Studies*, vol. 13
(April 1987), p. 355-71.
A study of the transformation of Ovimbundu peasant agriculture in response to the
demands of the colonial state. Until 1927, it is argued that Angola paralleled other
African states, and peasant production flourished. However, the subsequent imposition
of a system in which most Africans were placed in the category of forced labourers, led
to a collapse of the sector, although it never entirely disappeared.

412 **Política agrícola e participação camponesa na República Popular de
Angola: a região de Malange.** (Agrarian policy and peasant
participation in the People's Republic of Angola: the region of
Malanje.)
Lisbon: Centro de Informação e Difusão Amílcar Cabral (CIDAC),
1980. 166p. (Cadernos CIDAC, no. 5).
The introduction to this report focuses on colonial agriculture, subsequent developments in the zones liberated by the MPLA, and the first agrarian plans of the
Movement after independence. Then, MPLA policy is considered in more detail with
reference to the district of Malanje. There is an outline of the colonial legacy in the
region, the types of state enterprise attempted, and the difficulties encountered in
trying to establish a socialist agricultural system. Despite problems, it is argued that a
real participation of the masses in agricultural planning and decision-making has been
achieved in the region. The report is nonetheless limited, being based on a CIDAC
mission to the area, lasting only 'a few days', in January 1980.

413 **Primeiro seminário sobre cooperação agrícola.** (First seminar on
agrarian co-operation.)
Departamento de Educação Política e Ideológica do Comité Central do
MPLA-Partido do Trabalho. Luanda: Gráfica Popular, 1978. 46p.
Describes the structure of peasant agriculture in Angola during the colonial period,
and also in the zones liberated by the MPLA. This is followed by a discussion of the
need for agricultural co-operatives, and the role of the MPLA as a vanguard party in

establishing them. The document is available at the Centro de Informação e Difusão Amílcar Cabral in Lisbon (Ref A.Coop I.5).

414 **Programa piloto de extensão rural.** (Pilot programme of rural extension.)
Carlos Pombares, Benjamin Castello, José Amor. Luanda: Ministério de Agricultura, Programa de Extensão Rural, 1988. [n.p.]. bibliog.

A substantial report, providing a description of experiences in the pilot rural extension zone of Huíla district in the mid-1980s, and then outlining the proposed programme for rural extension in the country as a whole. A number of statistical tables are also included. It is available at the Centro de Informação e Difusão Amílcar Cabral (Ref. AO-Agr II.2).

415 **Recenseamento agrícola de Angola.** (Agricultural census of Angola.)
Luanda: Missão de Inquéritos Agrícolas de Angola, 1964-69. 23 vols.

An agricultural census, which is divided into volumes by geographical area and type of agriculture (capitalist, peasant, etc.). Also included are tables of the number of agricultural holdings, areas under different crops, livestock, farm labour, etc. as well as explanatory text (in Portuguese) and a number of useful maps.

416 **La reorganisation de l'agriculture en Angola comme phase de la transition: les cooperatives de production agricole.** (The reorganization of agriculture in Angola as a phase of transition: the agricultural production co-operatives.)
[Clara Gonçalves]. Louvain-la-Neuve, Belgium: Centre Tricontinental, 1981. 75p. maps.

An analysis of the attempt to transform Angolan agriculture along socialist lines in the immediate post-independence period. Part 1 starts with a discussion of pre-capitalist modes of production, and then considers the partial dissolution of these as capitalism penetrated the region. Using this as a historical base, part 2 then deals with specific socio-economic aspects of the transition to socialism in the agricultural sector, and in particular the attempts to establish agricultural production co-operatives. Difficulties encountered in this programme are blamed on insufficient organizational strength of the MPLA, as well as the colonial legacy, but the concept of co-operatives is hardly questioned.

417 **Sowing the seeds of failure: early Portuguese cotton cultivation in Angola and Mozambique, 1820-1926.**
M. Anne Pitcher. *Journal of Southern African Studies*, vol. 17, no. 1 (1991), p. 43-70.

Discusses abortive Portuguese attempts to establish cotton cultivation in Angola and Mozambique during the 19th century. Factors cited include natural conditions, fluctuations of international prices, confused colonial policy, inappropriate production methods and African resistance. Pitcher argues that the subsequent and infamous cotton regime of the *Estado Novo* in the 1930s learnt from earlier errors in its attempts to strictly control both prices and labour.

**Lista dos insectos com interesse económico em Angola.** (List of insects of economic importance in Angola.)
*See* item no. 48.

**Pouvoir populaire et cooperatives en Angola (1974-1977): cooperatives de consommation a Luanda et co-operatives de production a Malange.** (Popular power and co-operatives in Angola (1974-1977): consumer co-operatives in Luanda and production co-operatives in Malanje.)
*See* item no. 387.

**Estatísticas agrícolas correntes de Angola. 1972-1973.** (Current agricultural statistics of Angola. 1972-1973.)
*See* item no. 432.

# Transport and
# Communications

418  **Communications and hydraulic developments in Guinea, Angola and Moçambique.**
Ministry for Overseas Provinces.  Lisbon: General Overseas Agency, 1961. 80p.
Outlines development undertaken by the Portuguese in Angola and the two other colonies mentioned in the title, including construction of railways and roads, development of hydro-electic dams, and sea and airport improvements.

419  **Lombwelo: Línhas Aéreas de Angola.** (Lombwelo: Angolan Airlines.)
Luanda: TAAG Angolan Airlines, 1989- . bi-monthly.
The in-flight magazine of TAAG Angolan Airlines, providing news and views on air travel in and to Angola.

**Estatística dos Veículos Motorizados.** (Motorized vehicle statistics.)
*See* item no. 430.

# Employment, Labour and the Trade Unions

420 **A history of labour law in Angola.**
Frank Luce. LLM thesis, University of Toronto, Toronto, Canada.
1990. 222p. bibliog.

A comprehensive history of the labour law of Angola, which first provides a background to class formation and labour history in the country, and then examines historical changes in the law from the mid 19th century to the present day. It discusses colonial structures of the state, capital and labour, going on to focus on the transition from slavery to contract labour from 1850-1926; the proletarianization of the workforce up to 1961; and the changes brought about under the revised Rural Labour Code and later during the armed struggle. A final chapter examines changes since independence. The author argues that since the days of slavery, the international community has been a significant actor in influencing Angolan labour law. He argues for continued pressure, to ensure that the state meets ILO conventions and recommendations in the future, and does not allow the implementation of structural adjustment to prejudice the interests of labour.

421 **Labour in Portuguese West Africa.**
William A. Cadbury. London: Routledge; New York: E. P. Dutton,
1910. 2nd ed. 187p.

A classic study of slavery and its continuation in the contract labour system, which focuses on São Tomé e Príncipe, but includes one chapter on a visit to Angola, and in the first appendix, a report by Joseph Burtt and Dr W. C. Horton on their own visit to the interior of Angola, the main source of supply of slaves. Other appendices include translations of labour contracts, decrees, and statements by government officials on the trade. The book was reprinted in New York in 1969.

422  **A modern slavery.**
Henry W. Nevinson, with an introduction by Basil Davidson, 1963.
125p.

Originally published in 1906 (London: Harper & Bros), this is an account of the author's visit to Angola in 1904-5. It provides a factual picture of an economy based on forced labour. In the introduction to this edition, Basil Davidson highlights the maintenance of the 'slave' economy up to the 1960s, and cites this as essential background to the 1961 rebellion.

423  **Syndicalisme urbain, luttes ouvrières et questions ethniques: Luanda (Angola): 1974-77/1981. Notes sur une recherche.** (Urban trade unionism, workers struggles, and ethnic questions: Luanda [Angola]: 1974-77/1981.)
Michel Cahen.  Paris: CNRS, 1985. 29p. maps. (Journées d'Etude sur les Processus d'Urbanisation en Afrique).

An analysis of the development of the *União Nacional dos Trabalhadores Angolanos* (UNTA) in Luanda, and in particular, the ethnic problems it has faced. The work starts with an analysis of the ethnic structure of the population of Angola, and of the development of trade union militancy in general. Then specific issues are considered in more detail, including the differences between the '*poder popular*' (or people's power) movement, and the centralizing tendencies of the MPLA government, the manner in which the MPLA attempted to integrate the trade union movement, and the subsequent flight of some ethnic groups from that movement. It is argued that the MPLA needs to recognize the positive aspects of ethnicity in order to win back the confidence of many of these groups. The report is available at the Centro de Informação e Difusão Amílcar Cabral (Ref. A-T/S I.5), along with a number of other, unpublished documents and pamphlets on the trade union movement.

424  **Trabalho. Boletim, Ministério do Trabalho e Segurança Social.** (Labour. Bulletin of the Ministry of Labour and Social Security.)
Luanda: República Popular de Angola, 1981- . irregular.

A reasonably scholarly journal providing information on new legislation in the fields of employment and social services, as well as articles on labour issues, and reports of congresses. It continues a previous series published three times a year during the colonial era from 1963-74 (*Trabalho. Boletim do Instituto do Trabalho, Previdência e Acção Social.* [Employment. Bulletin of the Institute of Employment, Social Security and Social Work.]  Luanda: Institute of Employment, Social Security and Social Work.). More recent editions of the earlier title included a summary of each article in French and English.

# Statistics

425  **African Statistical Yearbook: Part 3: East and Southern Africa.**
New York: United Nations Economic Commission for Africa (ECA),
1976- . annual.
A reliable statistical digest based on ECA estimates as well as national and
international publications. Includes data on population, GDP/GNP, agriculture,
industry, transport and communications, foreign trade, and state budgets.

426  **Boletim Mensal de Estatística.** (Monthly statistical bulletin.)
Luanda: Direcção Provincial dos Serviços de Estatística, 1949-73.
monthly.
A statistical digest covering population, health, production, commerce, transport and
communications, credit and finance. First published by the Repartição Técnica de
Estatística Geral, from 1958-66 it was published by the Direcção dos Serviços de
Economia e Estatística Geral. In addition to other volumes listed in this bibliography,
the same service was also producing, by 1973, the following volumes which have not
been listed separately: *Anuário Estatístico* (Annual statistics); *Estatística Postal* (Postal
statistics); *Estatística de Prédios e Fogos* (Building and household statistics); and
*Legislação Estatística e Instruções* (Statistical legislation and instructions), each on an
annual basis. This statistical activity was brought to an end at independence.

427  **Estatística das Contribuições e Impostos.** (Tax and excise statistics.)
Luanda: Direcção Provincial dos Serviços de Estatística, 1951-68.
annual.
Annual statistics of finance in the colony of Angola.

428 **Estatística de Educação.** (Education statistics.)
Luanda: Direcção Provincial dos Serviços de Estatística, 1954-72.
annual.

Education statistics, including information on school enrolments, and infrastructural provision in education.

429 **Estatística do Comércio Externo.** (External trade statistics.)
Luanda: Direcção Provincial dos Serviços de Estatística, 1939-74.
annual.

Annual trade statistics of the colony of Angola in the post-war period. The title varied: for some years, for example, it was published as *Estatística do Comércio Externo e da Navegação* (Statistics of external trade and navigation), before a separate series, *Estatística de Navegação Marítima* (Maritime navigation statistics) was established.

430 **Estatística dos Veículos Motorizados.** (Motorized vehicle statistics.)
Luanda: Direcção Provincial dos Serviços de Estatística, 1967-73.

A relatively small volume detailing the registration of motor vehicles, as well as statistics on road accidents.

431 **Estatística Industrial.** (Industrial statistics.)
Luanda: Direcção dos Serviços de Estatística, 1965. 218p.

This one-off edition of industrial statistics provides information on industrial activity carried out in 1965, as well as time series data for the production of principal commodities, in most cases for 1960-65.

432 **Estatísticas agrícolas correntes de Angola. 1972-1973.** (Current agricultural statistics of Angola. 1972-1973.)
Luanda: Missão de Inquéritos Agrícolas de Angola, 1974. [n.p.]. maps.

A summary of agricultural statistics gathered in the agricultural census of 1973, concerning the 1972/73 growing season. Data is presented on the number and size of holdings, crops, livestock, and the occupation of farmers, and is subdivided for thirty-six zones, covering the whole country. Unsurprisingly, there are a number of gaps in certain regions, and the overall quality of the census can be questioned.

**Recenseamento agrícola de Angola.** (Agricultural census of Angola.)
*See* item no. 415.

# Planning and the Environment

433 **Angola.**
Otto Greyer. In: *Housing policies in the socialist Third World*. Edited by Kosta Mathéy. Munich: Profile; London, New York: Mansell, 1990, p. 129-145.
A discussion of organizational, political and architectural aspects of housing construction and management in post-independence Angola. It includes a section on self-help housing schemes.

434 **Angola: a situation report.**
Brian J. Huntley. *African Wildlife*, vol. 30, no. 1 (Jan. 1976), p. 10-14.
An outline of the history of nature conservation in Angola from colonial times through to the breakdown of policing against poachers immediately after independence. Subsequent to this article, large-scale killing of wild animals has led to depopulation of many species.

435 **The effects of guerilla warfare in Angola and Mozambique.**
Wolf Roder. *Antipode*, vol. 5, no. 2 (May 1973), p. 14-21.
This article reports on the independence struggle in Angola and Mozambique, before considering the environmental impact of Portuguese counter-insurgency operations, including defoliation and its human consequences. There is also a section on US involvement.

436 **Ensaio de um estudo geográfico da rede urbana de Angola.** (Analysis of a geographical study of the urban network of Angola.)
Ilídio do Amaral. Lisbon: Junta de Investigação do Ultramar, 1962. 99p. maps. (Estudos, Ensaios e Documentos, no. 97).
A short paper on the urban geography of Angola, based on a historical analysis of the origins and development of various Angolan cities, including Luanda and Benguela. Amongst other assertions, Amaral argues that their 'perfect racial integration' is a

product of their particular Portuguese history. Statistical data on urban populations is also included. There is a one-page English summary.

437 **A habitação tradicional angolana: aspectos da sua evolução.** (Traditional Angolan housing: aspects of its evolution.)
José Redinha.   Lisbon: CITA, Fundo de Turismo e Publicidade, 1973. 2nd ed. 53p. bibliog.
Describes traditional houses in Angola, including their construction, internal layout, materials used, etc. The evolution of housing forms from rural areas of the country to the *muceques* or shanties of Luanda is traced. The author argues that whilst nothing can be done about traditional rural homes, in Luanda, modern materials and ideas must be promoted as an alternative to traditional dwellings.

438 **Luanda e os seus '*muceques*': problemas de geográfia urbana.** (Luanda and its shanties: problems of urban geography.)
Ilídio do Amaral.   *Finisterra* (Lisbon), vol. 18, no. 36 (1983) p. 293-325.
A description of the development of the '*muceques*' or shanty towns of Luanda, especially their population and ethnic characteristics. Based on data from prior to independence, the article includes several maps and aerial photgraphs, and an interesting discussion of the white population of these areas. There is a not too informative English summary.

439 **Outlines of wildlife conservation in Angola.**
Brian J. Huntley.   *Journal of the Southern African Wildlife Management Association*, vol. 4 (1974), p. 157-66.
Provides a useful background to the physical geography of Angola, before discussing the role of conservation areas in protecting threatened ecosystems and endangered species. However, a fairly depressing picture is painted of the prospects for the implementation of such a conservation strategy in Angola.

**Luanda, Angola: the development of internal forms and functional patterns.**
*See* item no. 69.

# Education

440 **Colóquio sobre a educação e ciências humanas na Africa de língua portuguesa, 20-22 de janeiro de 1975.** (Conference on education and social science in Lusophone Africa, 20-22 January, 1975.)
Lisbon: Fundação Calouse Gulbenkian, 1979. 386p. bibliog.
This book provides the text of contribution by fourteen participants in this conference on the future of research and higher education in Lusophone Africa. The texts are in their original Portuguese, French or English, and cover five themes: the future for Portuguese language education; Portuguese contributions to the social sciences in Africa; social science courses in independent Africa; social science courses in Portuguese, Angolan and Mozambican universities; and the need for training of new teachers and social scientists.

441 **Education in Angola, 1878-1914: a history of culture transfer and administration.**
Michael Anthony Samuels. New York: Teachers College Press, 1970. 185p. maps. bibliog. (Teachers College Studies in Education).
An account of the development of education in Angola at the turn of the century. After a brief introduction to Portuguese involvement in Angola, and the 'aristocratic' educational heritage it had created by the middle of the 19th century, the book goes on to discuss major educational issues as Portuguese influence expanded, and the role of Christian missions in developing the education system. The failure of attempts to develop a provincial education policy, and the limited influence of both Catholic and Protestant missions are also discussed.

442 **Formação. Boletim do Conselho Nacional de Formação Profissional.**
(Training. Bulletin of the National Council for Professional Training.)
Luanda: Comissão Permanente da Conselho Nacional de Formação Profissional, 1989- . irregular.
A magazine aimed at those training professionals.

443  **Mozambique and Angola: reconstruction in the social sciences.**
Bertil Egerö.  Uppsala, Sweden: Scandinavian Institute of African
Studies, 1977. 78p. (Scandinavian Institute of African Studies Research
Report, no. 42).
A review of the state of the social sciences in higher education establishments in
Angola and Mozambique after independence, with an assessment of the prospects for
development of both teaching and research in the field. The study concentrates on
Mozambique, where at the time of writing, the planning process for education was
more advanced. Chapters 6 and 7 focus on Angola, and outline major debates and
government thinking on higher education in general.

444  **Portuguese colonialism in Africa: the end of an era. The effects of
Portuguese colonialism on education, science, culture and information.**
Eduardo de Sousa Ferreira.  Paris: UNESCO, 1974. 170p.
Written before the 1974 coup in Portugal, this short book provides a fairly
comprehensive survey of the social and cultural legacy of Portuguese rule throughout
its African territories. After a brief historical introduction, chapter 2 examines the
history of education, including the role of missionary organizations and the educational
reforms of the 1960s. This is followed by a short assessment of the clash of European
and African cultures, covering the assimilation policy and the culture of African
resistance. Finally, a chapter on information examines the state of newspapers, radio,
television and cinemas at the end of the Portuguese era. The book is supported
throughout by detailed statistical tables, which include data specifically on Angola.

**Umbundu kinship and character.**
*See* item no. 164.

**Estatística de Educação.** (Education statistics.)
*See* item no. 428.

# Literature

445 **Africa: Literatura, Arte e Cultura.** (Africa: Literature, Art and
  Culture.)
  Linda-a-Velha, Portugal: ALAC, 1978- . quarterly.
An arts magazine dealing mainly with Lusophone Africa, including Angola. Includes
news and criticism, as well as original poems and stories.

446 **African writers in Portuguese.**
  Mário António Fernandes de Oliveira. *African Arts/Arts d'Afrique*,
  vol. 3, no. 2 (winter 1970), p. 80-84.
Describes the development of African literature in the Portuguese colonies, including
the rise of literary movements, and the role of reaction to, and imitation of,
Portuguese writing.

447 **Angola: um encontro com escritores.** (Angola: a meeting with writers.)
  Michel Laban. Lisbon: Fundação Eng. António de Almeida, 1991.
  2 vols.
An interesting volume containing interviews with 22 contemporary Angolan writers,
mostly carried out by the author during a visit to Luanda in 1988. The interviews cover
a range of topics, from literature to politics, and provide an unrivalled biographical
portrait of the most important Angolan authors of today, including a number of
younger writers. Volume 1 covers interviews with Oscar Ribas, Raúl David, Aires de
Almeida Santos, Uanhenga Xitu, António Jacinto, David Van-Dunem, Antero Abreu,
Henriques Abranches, António Cardoso, Mário António, José Luandino Vieira,
Manuel dos Santos Lima and Fernando Costa Andrade. Volume 2 covers Arnaldo
Santos, Arlindo Barbeita, Jofre Rocha, Ruy Duarte de Carvalho, Manuel Rui, Jorge
Macedo, Pepetela, Boaventura Cardoso, and Paula Tavares. Each volume contains an
author and subject index.

448   **Archote. Chama Jovem da Literatura Angolana.** (Torch. The Young
Call of Angolan Literature.)
Luanda: Amizade Canteiro Novo, 1986-87. quarterly.

One of a number of publications that provided, at various times, a vehicle for new
Angolan literature. Several issues are held by the Centro de Informação e Difusão
Amílcar Cabral in Lisbon, and these include poems and short stories by mainly young
Angolan writers. Another, similar magazine was '*Aspiração: Folheto de Cultura, Arte e
Literatura*' (Desire: Pamphlet of Culture, Art and Literature), which was first
published in 1982.

449   **Black mind: a history of African literature.**
Oscar Ronald Dathorne.   Minneapolis, Minnesota: University of
Minnesota Press, 1974. 527p. bibliog.

This major work on the history of Black African literature contains a useful chapter on
African literature in Portuguese, which discusses the politics of prose and poetry
writings in the former Portuguese colonies, including Angola. Elsewhere in the book,
there are also several references to Angolan oral traditions of storytelling.

450   **Chief Xa-Mucuari's grievance.**
Castro Soromenho.   In: *Africa in prose*. Edited by O. R. Dathorne,
Willfried Feuser.   Harmondsworth, England: Penguin, 1969, p. 227-
32.

An extract from the romantic novel *Terra morta* (Lisbon: Sá da Costa Editora, 1960.
261p.), which paints a vivid portrait of life in a provincial Angolan town during the
colonial era. The novel has been translated into French, as well as Czech, Russian,
German and Hungarian, but not yet into English. Soromenho, a white journalist, was
born in Mozambique, but lived and worked for many years in Angola. His work is also
considered in an article by Raymond L. Moloney, entitled 'Castro Soromenho's Africa'
(In: *Studies in honor of Lloyd A. Kasten*.   Madison, Wisconsin: Hispanic Seminar of
Medieval Studies, 1975, p. 175-84.).

451   **Critical perspectives on Lusophone literature from Africa.**
Edited by Donald Burness.   Washington, DC: Three Continents,
1981. 307p. bibliog.

A collection of essays dealing with literature in the five Lusophone countries of Africa.
After two general chapters, five are devoted directly to Angola. These cover the rôle
of oral traditions and the liberation struggle in Angolan writing, as well as discussions
of the work of two white Angolans, Luandino Vieira and Castro Soromenho, and the
leader of the MPLA, Agostinho Neto. In part 2 of the book, there are two further
chapters on Angola, written in Portuguese, concerning Angolan creole writing, and the
anti-apartheid stance of Luandino Vieira. Finally, in part 3, four Portuguese language
journals published in Luanda - *Mensagem*, the journal of the '*Vamos descobrir Angola*'
(Let's discover Angola) group; as well as *Cultura*, *Convivium*, and *Vector*, are
reviewed, again in Portuguese. Each chapter in parts 2 and 3 contains an English
summary.

# Literature

452 **Early literary reactions to the Portuguese presence in Angola.**
Janet Elizabeth Carter. *African Studies*, vol. 49, no. 1 (1990),
p. 49-58.
Situates early colonial literature within Angolan literature in general, and then
proceeds to classify it as either 'proto-nationalist', or 'colonialist', i.e. as upholding or
accepting the colonial system. The article covers journalism as well as mainstream
literary writings.

453 **The emergence of African literature in Portuguese.**
Wilfried Feuser, Isa Maria Drummond Simões. *Nsukka Studies in
African Literature* (Nigeria), vol. 4 (1986), p. 73-100.
An analysis of Afro-Portuguese literature, and its themes of negritude, mulatism,
tropicalism, negrism and indigenism. It is argued that this literature began to develop
six decades before African writing in English or French, and that by the 1960s, its
poetry had acheived a 'vast and complex objective totality'. As well as a general
analysis, a section of the article deals specifically with Angolan writers.

454 **Espontaneidades da minha alma.** (Spontaneities of my soul.)
José da Silva Maia Ferreira. Lisbon: Edições 70, 1980. 2nd ed. 139p.
bibliog.
This collection of over fifty poems was the first literary work to be published in
Lusophone Africa (Luanda: Imprensa do Governo, 1849). The author was a *mestiço*
Angolan. The modern edition includes an introduction by Gerald Moser, also in
Portuguese.

455 **Essays in Portuguese-African literature.**
Gerald Moser. Philadelphia: Pennsylvania State University,
Administrative Committee on Research, 1969. 88p. map. (Pennsylvania
State University Studies, no. 26).
Four essays on literature from and about Portuguese Africa. The first three deal with
general themes: the origin of literature in the Portuguese African colonies; a
description of the main literary trends and movements by region; and an examination
of the importance of African themes in work by native Portuguese writers. The final
chapter is an appreciation of the work of the Angolan author, Castro Soromenho. An
appendix includes a number of short poems and prose texts written by authors
reviewed in the essays, with translations into English.

456 **50 poetas africanos: Angola, Moçambique, Guiné-Bissau, Cabo Verde,
São Tomé e Principe.** (50 African poets: Angola, Mozambique, Guinea-
Bissau, Cape Verde, São Tomé e Principe).
Edited by Manuel Ferreira. Lisbon: Plátono, 1989. 487p.
For a full appreciation of Angolan poetry, it is necessary to read it in the original
Portuguese. Fifteen Angolan poets are featured in this recent anthology of African
poems in Portuguese, which focuses in detail on the themes of individual authors, and
includes poems from the post-independence era. In contrast, the editor's previous
volume, *No reino de Caliban: antologia panorámica da poesia africana de expressão
portuguesa. Tom. 2: Angola, São Tomé e Principe* (In the reign of Caliban: panoramic
anthology of African poetry in Portuguese. Vol. 2: Angola, São Tomé e Principe.

Lisbon: Seara Nova, 1976. 489p.) aimed to cover a wide range of authors, stretching from the early work of Geraldo Bessa Victor, through to poems from the 1970s by David Mestre, Jofre Rocha and Arlindo Barbeitos. Another useful Portuguese language anthology is Mário de Andrade's *Antologia temática de poesia africana* (Thematic anthology of African poetry. Lisbon: Sá da Costa, 1976-79. 2 vols) which covers from 1930 to the present day, and includes biographical notes and some criticism.

### 457 Fire: six writers from Angola, Mozambique and Cape Verde.

Donald Burness. Washington, DC: Three Continents Press, 1977. 148p. bibliog.

Six critical essays on writers from the former Portuguese colonies in Africa, of whom four, José Luandino Vieira, Agostinho Neto, Geraldo Bessa Victor, and Mário António, are from Angola. A further chapter includes eight poems by Bessa Victor, alongside English translations by the author of the volume, whilst an afterword is written by the Portuguese critic, Manuel Ferreira.

### 458 Five Angolan poets.

Ann Titterington. *The London Magazine*, vol. 2, no. 7 (July 1962), p. 35-43.

An introduction to, and English translation of, poems by Costa Andrade, Mário António, António Cardoso, Arnaldo Santos and Agostinho Neto.

### 459 A horse of white clouds: poems from Lusophone Africa.

Selected and translated from the Portuguese by Donald Burness. Athens, Ohio: Ohio University Press, 1989. 193p.

An anthology of poetry from Lusophone Africa, of particular interest since it includes the original Portuguese text alongside each English translation. Fifteen Angolan writers are included; alongside authors relatively well-known to an English-speaking audience, such as Geraldo Bessa Victor, Agostinho Neto and António Jacinto, are more recent writers such as Arlindo Barbeitos, David Mestre and Carlos Ferreira. Also included is one poem by Joaquim Cordeiro da Matta (1857-94), one of the first Angolans to encourage the development of a specifically Angolan literature.

### 460 Lord of darkness.

Robert Silverberg. London: Victor Gollancz; New York: Ann Arbor House, 1983. 558p.

A novel based on the life of English seaman Andrew Battell in Portuguese West Africa. Whilst following broadly the story of his 'adventures' (*see The Strange adventures of Andrew Battell of Leigh in Angola and the adjoining regions* [q.v.]), much of the detail of Battell's character is sketched in by the author.

### 461 Lotus: Afro-Asian writings.

Berlin: Association of Afro-Asiatic Writers, vols. 40/41, (April-Sept. 1979), 117p.

A special issue devoted to literature and art from Angola, and prepared for the 6th Congress of the Asssociation of Afro-Asiatic Writers in Luanda, by the *União dos Escritores Angolanos* and the *União dos Artistas Angolanos*. It includes essays by

# Literature

Agostinho Neto and Henrique Guerra; stories by Oscar Ribas, Raul David, José Luandino Vieira and Pepetela; and poems by Agostinho Neto, António Jacinto, Eugénia Neto, Costa Andrade, António Cardoso, Manuel Rui, Cochat Osório, and Ruy Duarte de Carvalho, all translated into English, with a preface by Jofre Rocha.

## 462 The loves of João Vêncio.
José Luandino Vieira, translated from the Portuguese by Richard Zenith. London, New York: Harcourt Brace Jovanovich, 1991. 64p.
First published in 1979 as *João Vêncio, os seus amores* (Lisbon: Edições 70), this novel tells of the events leading to the imprisonment of a *mestiço* youth for murder. It provides a flavour of the seedier side of life in a shanty town. In its original form, it blended Portuguese and Kimbundu to reflect the language of the *muceques*; the English translation tries to mirror the disjointed nature of the narrative.

## 463 Luuanda.
José Luandino Vieira, translated from the Portuguese by Tamara L. Bender, with Donna S. Hill. London: Heinemann, 1980. 118p. (African Writers Series, no. 222).
Three short stories based on life in the *muceques* or shanties of Luanda, which provide a vivid portrait of slum communities under the all-pervading influence of Portuguese rule. They were written whilst the author was in prison, and when they received the Grand Prize for fiction from the *Sociedade Portuguesa de Escritores* in 1965, both the book and the society were quickly banned. A second edition, which appeared after the author's release in 1972 (Lisbon: Edições 70), was also banned, and the book was not widely available until after the 1974 revolution. 'Luuanda' is the Kimbundu pronunciation of Luanda. The stories are written in the author's characteristic style, based on the fusion of Portuguese and Kimbundu spoken in the capital. The translation seeks to reflect its unusual and difficult construction. Another novel written by Luandino in jail in 1967 and first published as *Nós, os do Makulusu* (We, of Makulusu. Lisbon: Edições 70, 1974) is available in French translation (*Nous autres, de Makulusu*. Paris: Gallimard, 1989. 148p.). It deals with the friendship of four boys, two white, one mulatto and one black, during the anti-colonial struggle of the 1960s.

## 464 *Luz e Crença*: an episode in Angolan journalism.
Manuel Ferreira, translated from the Portuguese by Julia Perkins. *Portuguese Studies*, vol. 1 (1985), p. 168-81.
Examines the birth of national consciousness in Angolan literature through an analysis of the early 20th century social and literary journal published in Luanda, *Luz e Crença*.

## 465 Manuel Rui's *Sim camarada!*: interpolation and the transformation of narrative discourse.
Phyllis Reisman Butler. *Callaloo* (Baltimore), vol. 14, no. 2 (spring 1991), p. 307-12.
A critical account of the work of Manuel Rui Alves Monteiro, a former MPLA Minister for Information in the Angolan transitional government after independence. It is preceeded, on p. 291-306, by a short story from his collection *Sim camarada!*, entitled 'The Watch' (*O relógio*), translated by Ronald W. Sousa. The story tells of a

watch taken from a dead Portuguese soldier, and later exchanged for the lives of MPLA prisoners.

466 **Mayombe: a novel of the Angolan struggle.**
Pepetela (Artur Carlos Mauricio Pestana dos Santos), translated from the Portuguese by Michael Wolfers. London: Heinemann; Harare: Zimbabwe Publishing House, 1983. 184p. (African Writers Series).

This novel centres on the activities of a unit of guerilla fighters of the MPLA in the enclave province of Cabinda in the early 1970s, and at their base camp in the neighbouring Congo republic. It is a frank and gripping account of the political, ethnic and sexual tensions created within the MPLA and its units during the war, as well as a perceptive and moving portrait of the unit's commander. Pepetela himself served with the guerillas in Cabinda. Although the book was written during the struggle, the original was not published until after independence (*Mayombe*. Lisbon: Edições 70, 1980. 286p.). It won the National Prize for Literature in 1980, and was subsequently made into a film under the direction of Rui Guerra.

467 **Monte Gracioso, and other poems.**
António Jacinto, translated from the Portuguese by Don Burness.
*Okike* (Nigeria), vol. 27/28 (1988), p. 119-22.

Four recent poems by Jacinto, entitled 'Monte Gracioso', 'Oh if you could see here poetry that does not exist', 'Memories and longings', and 'The rhythm of the tomtom', each in English translation.

468 **Negritude as a theme in the poetry of the Portuguese-speaking world.**
Richard Preto-Rodas. Gainesville, Florida: University of Florida Press, 1970. 85p. (University of Florida Humanities Monographs Series, no. 31).

After an introductory chapter that outlines the major motifs of negritude as a theme in poetry, three chapters examine the theme in work respectively from Brazil, the Atlantic Islands, and Angola and Mozambique. The latter chapter includes discussion of the work of Mário de Andrade, Geraldo Bessa Victor, António Jacinto and Agostinho Neto. The appendix examines linguistic differences of African and Brazilian Portuguese from that of mainland Portugal, and how these affect poetic rhythm.

469 **Ngunga's adventures: a story of Angola.**
Pepetela, translated from the Portuguese by Chris Searle. London: Young World, 1980. 63p.

Written in 1972, this is the story of a child learning about life and the liberation struggle in Angola towards the end of Portuguese occupation. The text, which in its English version is aimed at schoolchildren, is accompanied by numerous illustrations by Steve Lee, as well as photographs of Angola.

# Literature

470 **On literature and national culture.**
Agostinho Neto, translated from the Portuguese by Russell Hamilton.
Luanda: Angolan Writers Union, 1979. 30p. (Cadernos Lavra e
Oficina, no. 20).

A short pamphlet containing three keynote speeches by Agostinho Neto made to the
Angolan Writers Union (*União dos Escitores Angolanos*) between 1975-79, each
calling on writers to help to raise national consciousness.

471 **Poems from Angola.**
Selected, translated from the Portuguese, and introduced by Michael
Wolfers. London: Heinemann, 1979. 112p. (African Writers Series,
no. 215).

An anthology of fifty poems by some twenty-two Angolan poets translated into
English, including a number by Agostinho Neto and Arlindo Barbeitos. The poems
date from the late-1940s, and the cultural movement associated with the student
slogan, '*Vamos descobrir Angola*' (Let's discover Angola) through to post-independence writings. A short introduction and biographical notes are included by the editor.

472 **Quando a terra voltar a sorrir um dia.** (When the land begins to smile
again one day.)
Jonas Malheiro Savimbi. Lisbon: Perspectivas e Realidades, 1985.
110p.

An anthology of poems penned by the UNITA leader, Jonas Savimbi, between 1965-
81. Many deal with the continuing struggle of UNITA, praising comrades in arms and
designed to inspire confidence. Others reflect on Savimbi's own past, and his vision of
a future Angola under UNITA control.

473 **Queen Nzinga in fact and fiction.**
Gerald Max Joseph Moser. In: *Neo-African literature and culture:
essays in memory of Janheinz Jahn.* Edited by B. Lindfors, Ulla
Schild. Wiesbaden, Germany: B. Heymann, 1976, p. 220-42.

An analysis of literature inspired by the reign of Queen Jinga of Matamba, from the
biography written by her confessor, Father António da Gaeta in 1660, to the romance
of M. P. Pacavira in 1975.

474 **The real life of Domingos Xavier.**
José Luandino Vieira, translated from the Portuguese by Michael
Wolfers. London: Heinemann, 1978. 84p. (African Writers Series,
no. 202).

Set in Angola in 1960, this novel tells the story of the arrest and torture of a tractor-
driver with progressive political sympathies, as well as the attempts of Luanda's
opposition movement, and the man's wife, to discover his whereabouts. Written in
1961, it was not published until 1971, and then in French. The original Portuguese
version first appeared after the 1974 Revolution (*A vida verdadeira de Domingos
Xavier*, Lisbon: Edições 70, 1974. 128p.).

130

475   **Sacred hope.**
Agostinho Neto, translated from the Portuguese, and introduced by
Marga Holness.   Dar-es-Salaam: Tanzania Publishing House, 1974.
84p.
An anthology of poems by Angola's best-known poet, and MPLA leader, Agostinho
Neto. Written between 1945-60, they tell of the hardships, and growth of political
consciousness of the Angolan people under colonial rule. A background to Neto's
poetry is provided by the translator. The anthology first appeared as an Italian
translation, entitled *Con occhi asciutti* (With dry eyes. Milan: Il Saggiatore, 1963), and
has subsequently been translated into French, Serbo-Croat, Russian and Chinese. The
most recent version in the original Portuguese, entitled *Sagrada esperança: poemas*
(Sacred hope: poems) was published in 1987 (Lisbon: Sá da Costa).

476   **The short stories of Geraldo Bessa Victor.**
Donald Burness.   *Ba Shiru*, vol. 6, no. 1 (spring 1974), p. 42-55.
Discusses the themes of Bessa Victor's writing, including race prejudice, cultural
schizophrenia, illicit sexuality between white and black, and the authenticity of
indigenous African culture. Also includes several poems, translated by Burness. *Ba
Shiru* was published by the Department of African Languages and Literature at the
University of Wisconsin-Madison.

477   **South of nowhere.**
António Lobo Antunes, translated from the Portuguese by Elizabeth
Lowe.   London: Chatto & Windus, 1983. 154p. maps.
The author of this novel served as a doctor on the Portuguese eastern front in Angola
in 1971-72. The story consists of reflections on this tour of duty in Angola, as narrated
to a woman in a Lisbon bar. It provides a vivid description of the frustration of troops
fighting against the 'invisible enemy' of the MPLA. First published in 1979 as *Os cus de
Judas* (Lisbon: Publicações Dom Quixote.).

478   **To name the wrong.**
W. S. Mervin.   In: *Introduction to African literature: an anthology of
critical writing from 'Black Orpheus'*. Edited by Ulli Beier.   London:
Longmans; Evanston, Illionis: Northwestern University Press, 1967,
p. 132-38.
Includes English translations of four poems by Agostinho Neto, first published in *Black
Orpheus* (no. 15 [1964], p. 34-37).

479   **Voices from an empire: a history of Afro-Portuguese literature.**
Russell G. Hamilton.   Minneapolis, Minnesota: University of
Minnesota Press, 1975. 450p. bibliog. (Minnesota Monographs in the
Humanities, no. 8).
The main English-language source of literary criticism on Portuguese African
literature, this work focuses on the main literary movements in Portugal's African
colonies on the eve of independence. The central concepts of Afro-Portuguese literature –
Lusotropicalism, negritude, and relations with Portugal and Brazil, are discussed. The
first five chapters focus on Angola, covering the social and cultural background to

# Literature

Angolan writing; initial colonial and settler literature; the '*Vamos descobrir Angola*' (Let's discover Angola) movement which reacted against the colonial agenda for literature; and finally poetry and prose literature respectively in modern Angola. The book argues that the literature of Angola is more strongly regionalist than in the other former Portuguese colonies. Includes a full bibliography of literature and criticism in Portuguese, divided by country.

480 **When bullets begin to flower: poems of resistance from Angola, Mozambique and Guiné.**
Selected and translated from the Portuguese by Margaret Dickinson. Nairobi: East African Publishing House, 1972. 131p. (Poets of Africa, no. 3).

An anthology of poems from Portuguese Africa, translated into English, which includes over forty by Angolan writers. A number of these are by Agostinho Neto and António Jacinto, whilst there are also individual contributions by Fernando Costa Andrade, Viriato da Cruz, Helder Neto, Arnaldo Santos, and Aires de Almeida Santos. The poems reflect life in the colony both before and during the struggle, and are accompanied by an introduction to the history of colonial rule and armed resistance. Translations of four poems by Neto and Jacinto also appear in Gerald Moore and Ulli Beier's English-language anthology *Modern poetry from Africa* (Harmondsworth, England: Penguin, 1973), whilst the work of Neto, Jacinto, Geraldo Bessa Victor, and Paço d'Arcos is also included, again in English translation, in *The penguin book of southern African verse* (Edited by Stephen Gray. Harmondsworth, England: Penguin, 1989).

481 **The world of 'mestre' Tamoda.**
Uanhenga Xitu (Agostinho Mendes de Carvalho), translated from the Portuguese by Annella McDermott. London: Readers International, 1988. 158p.

A superb book of short stories, in which 'mestre', or master, Tamoda displays his eloquence in Portuguese, faithfully learnt from the dictionary, and achieves fame for his rhetorical ability. The comic flavour of the stories is underpinned by a ridiculing of Portuguese society and values. The first story was written in prison, and first published in Angola as *Mestre Tamoda* (Luanda: União dos Escritores Angolanos, 1974). The remaining stories, which tell of Tamoda's continuing adventures in Luanda, and back in his rural village, were published as *Os discursos de mestre Tamoda* (The speeches of 'mestre' Tamoda) again by the União dos Escritores Angolanos, in 1984.

**Estudos Portugueses e Africanos.** (Portuguese and African Studies.)
*See* item no. 536.

**Lavra e Oficina.** (Work and workplace.)
*See* item no. 539.

# Arts and Customs

## Visual art

482  **Art Bakongo: les centres de style.** (Bakongo art: style centres.)
Raoul Leuhuard.   Arnouville-lès-Gonesse, France: *Arts d'Afrique Noire*, 1989. 2 vols. maps. (Supplement to vol. 55).
This major work, published as a supplement to the journal *Arts d'Afrique Noire*, provides a discussion of the origin and distribution of Bakongo art, dividing it into fifteen separate 'style centres'. Three of these are inside Angola: two, the Woyo-Kakongo (centred on Cabinda) and the Zombo-Sosso-Nkanu (centred on Mbanza-Kongo) are dealt with in the first volume, whilst another, the Solongo (centred on Ambriz) is considered in volume 2. Volume 1 also includes discussion of the origin of the Kongo kingdom, the anthropology of the Bakongo, and the work of artists in the region as a whole. There are many black-and-white photographs, depicting sculpture from the region.

483  **Art from the frontline: contemporary art from southern Africa.**
London: Frontline States/Karia Press, 1990 128p. bibliog.
A section on Angola includes two short texts respectively on Angolan art in general, and Angolan textile weaving, followed by six photographs of material included in the 'Frontline States' exhibition that toured the United Kingdom in 1990. There is also a foreword by the Angolan Secretary of State for Culture, Boaventura Cardoso.

484  **Art of central Africa: selected works of art from central Africa in the Ethnographical Department of the Danish National Museum.**
J. Nicholousen, Jens Yde.   Copenhagen: Danish National Museum, 1972. 92p. maps. bibliog.
Although mostly covering Congo and Zaïre , this book includes two colour plates of sculpture from the Bapende and Batshioko peoples of northeast Angola. Both artefacts are chairs. The text is in Danish and English.

485 **Collecting African art.**
Werner Gillon. London: Studio Vista/Christie's, 1979. 183p. maps.
bibliog.
Includes a short discussion of the main forms of collectable art from Angola, as well as
several illustrations of Chokwe masks.

486 **Desenhos na areia dos quiocos do nordeste de Angola.** (Sand drawings of
the Chokwe of northeast Angola.)
Mário Fontinha. Lisbon: Instituto de Investigação Científica Tropical,
1983. 304p. maps. bibliog. (Estudos, Ensaios e Documentos, no. 143).
Provides depiction and commentary on around 400 sand drawings as well as discussion
of the techniques of drawing, and the significance of this ephemeral art.

487 **Escultura africana em Portugal.** (African sculpture in Portugal.)
Ernesto Veiga de Oliveira. Lisbon: Instituto de Investigação
Científica Tropical, Museu de Etnologia, 1985. 153p.
Catalogue for a major exhibition of African sculpture in Lisbon, containing black-and-
white photographs of 153 exhibits, a number of these from various parts of Angola.
There is also a discussion of the history of African art in Portugal in French and
Portuguese.

488 **Les sculptures Tshokwé.** (Chokwe sculptures.)
Marie-Louise Bastin. Meudon, France: Alain et Françoise Chaffin,
1982. 291p. maps. bibliog.
An updated version of an earlier book, *Art decoratif Tshokwé* (Chokwe decorative
art), drawing on the author's PhD thesis. This volume includes ethnographic
information on the Chokwe, a detailed discussion of iconography, and aesthetics, and a
stylistic classification of Chokwe sculpture. These are followed by photographs of over
200 sculptures held in museums in various parts of Europe. Included are both
ceremonial regalia associated with various chiefdoms, and more common objects.
There is a glossary of African terms. The text is in French and English.

489 **Paredes pintadas da Lunda.** (Lunda house paintings.)
José Redinha. Lisbon: Companhia de Diamantes de Angola
(Diamang), 1953. 32p. (Museu do Dundo, Subsídios para a História,
Arqueologia e Etnografia dos Povos da Lunda, Publicações Culturais,
no. 18).
Contains colour plates of more than fifty examples of designs and paintings from the
walls of houses amongst the Lunda people of northeastern Angola. The work, by the
Director of the Dundo Museum, is preceeded by a short discussion in Portuguese of
the origin of such paintings in traditional sand drawings, and includes numerous plates
and photographs. A review of the book by M. C. Burkitt appeared in *Nature*, vol. 173
(Feb. 1954), p. 239-30.

490 **Peoples and cultures.**
Overseas Museum of Ethnology. Lisbon: Junta de Investigações
Científicas do Ultramar, 1972. [n.p.]. maps. bibliog.
A catalogue of artefacts collected from around the world by Portuguese ethnologists,
and exhibited at the National Gallery of Modern Art in Lisbon in 1972. Includes
descriptions, and many photographs, of over 600 exhibits, of which 183 were from
Angola.

491 **Statuettes Tshokwé du héros civilisateur 'Tshibinda Ilunga': à propos de
statuettes tshokwé représentant un chef chasseur.** (Chokwe statues of
the civilising hero 'Tshibinda Ilunga': concerning Chokwe statues
representing a hunting chief.)
Marie-Louise Bastin. Arnouville-lès-Gonesse, France: *Arts d'Afrique
Noire*, 1978. 128p. maps. bibliog. (Supplement to vol.19 [1976]).
This special edition of *Arts d'Afrique Noire* discusses Chokwe wood sculptures which
depict the hunting chief, and founder of a Lunda dynasty, Tshibinda Ilunga. The work
includes discussion of the historical foundation of the dynasty, and traditions
surrounding hunting activities in the region, before describing particular sculptures.
There are numerous black-and-white illustrations.

**In pursuit of a chameleon: early ethnographic photography from Angola in
context.**
*See* item no. 158.
**African folktales and sculpture.**
*See* item no. 503.

# Theatre and film

492 **Cinema angolana.** (Angolan cinema.)
Lisbon: Cinemática Portuguesa, 1987. 31p.
A programme produced to accompany a season of thirteen Angolan films shown at the
*Cinemática Portuguesa* in September 1987. A short article by M. S. Fonseca sets the
background to Angolan cinema, whilst another by José Maria Abrantes, written in
1985, examines the development and future of the film industry of Angola. Abrantes
paints a depressing picture of disinterest amongst official bodies, after a promising start
after independence.

493 **Sub-saharan African films and filmmakers: an annotated bibliography.**
Nancy Schmidt. London: Hans Zell, 1988. 401p. bibliog.
Includes over 50 references to Angolan films or filmmakers.

# Music

494 **African space/time concepts and the *tusona* ideographs in Luchazi culture, with a discussion of possible cross-parallels in music.**
Gerhard Kubik. *African Music*, vol. 6, no. 4 (1987), p. 53-89.
An analysis of the *tusona* tradition of writing found in pre-colonial times in much of eastern Angola, as well as parts of neighbouring Zambia and Zaïre, although now much more restricted. Parallels are drawn between the structure of this writing, in the form of ideographs, and musical structures from the wider Bantu-speaking area.

495 **Angolan traits in black music, games and dances of Brazil: a study of African cultural extensions overseas.**
Gerhard Kubik. Lisbon: Junta de Investigações Científicas do Ultramar, Centro de Estudos de Antropologia Cultural, 1979. 55p. (Estudos de Antropologia Cultural, no. 10).
An analysis of the Angolan origins of Brazilian music based on field research in both countries. Rhythms, dances and instruments that were transfered from Angola to Brazil are identified. A number of photographs of dances and instruments are included from both sides of the Atlantic.

496 **Folclore musical de Angola: colecção de fitas magnéticas e discos. I: Povo Quioco, Area de Lóvua, Lunda.** (Angolan folk music: collection of tapes and records. I: Chokwe people, Lóvua area, Lunda District.)
Companhia de Diamantes de Angola (Diamang), Serviços Culturais. Lisbon: Diamang, Serviços Culturais/Museu de Dundo, 1961. 276p.
Background notes in Portuguese and English for a set of tapes and records of music from Lunda District in northeast Angola, collected by Diamang, the state diamond-mining company. The first of two volumes (the second covers the Camissombo area of the same district), the book contains explanatory notes, details of musical instruments, photographs, musical analyses and the lyrics of the songs recorded. The music itself is available at the National Sound Archive, 29 Exhibition Road, London SW7, the Library of Congress, Folklore Division, Washington, DC, and the Peabody Museum of Archaeology and Ethnology, Harvard University, Cambridge, Massachussets.

497 **The Himba trumpet.**
Gordon D. Gibson. *Man*, vol. 62, no. 258 (Nov. 1962), p. 161-63.
A detailed description of a wax-bulbed trumpet as made by the Himba people, who live on either side of the Angola/Namibia border along the Cunene river. The article includes several photographs.

498 **Instrumentos musicais de Angola: sua construção e descrição. Notas históricas e etno-sociológicas da música angolana.** (Musical instruments of Angola: their construction and description. Historical and ethno-sociological notes on Angolan music.) José Redinha. Coimbra, Portugal: Instituto de Antropologia, Universidade de Coimbra, 1984. 230p. bibliog. (Publicações do Centro de Estudos Africanos, no. 3).
A survey of Angolan musical instruments, which deals with their construction, typology, distribution, and ethnic and sociological importance. There is a useful index of specialist terms, and a number of photographs and line drawings of individual instruments.

499 **Likembe tunings of Kufuna Kandonga.** Gerhard Kubik. *African Music*, vol. 6, no. 1 (1980), p. 70-88.
A measurement and analysis of the tuning of the *likembe*, a traditional Angolan instrument, as practiced by Kufuna Kandonga, a musician from Cuando-Cubango district. The tunings were originally recorded by the author in 1965.

500 **Música tradicional e aculturada dos !Kung' de Angola: uma introdução ao instrumentação, estrutura e técnicas de execução da música dos !Kung', incidindo em especial nos factores psicológico-sociais da actual mudança na cultura dos povos Khosian.** (Traditional and acculturated music of the !Kung' of Angola: an introduction to the instrumentation, structure and playing techniques of !Kung' music, focusing especially on psycho-social factors in the current evolution of the culture of Khosian peoples.) Gerhard Kubik, translated from the German by João de Freitas Branco. Lisbon: Junta de Investigações Científicas do Ultramar, 1970. 88p. bibliog. (Estudos de Antropoligia Cultural, no. 4).
Describes the musical instruments of the !Kung' peoples living around Cuito Cuanavale, including musical bows, wooden zithers, and other adopted instruments. There is also a section on dance, and numerous photographs are also included.

501 **Musical bows in south-western Angola.** Gerhard Kubik. *African Music*, vol. 5, no. 4 (1975/76), p. 98-104.
Describes musical bows collected and taped during a one-week visit to southwestern Angola by the author in 1965. Three types of bow are identified, and their use explained.

502 **Stern's guide to contemporary African music.** Ronnie Graham. London: Pluto, 1989. 2nd ed. 315p.
A short summary of Angolan traditional and popular music is provided on p. 221-25 of this Africa-wide review.

Arts and Customs. Folklore and customs

**Patterns of body movement in the music of boy's initiation in south-east Angola.**
*See* item no. 509.

# Folklore and customs

503 **African folktales and sculpture.**
Edited by Paul Radin. New York: Pantheon, 1952. 355p. maps.
(Bollingen Series, no. 32).
This volume of 81 stories and 132 illustrations of African sculptures contains one Mbundu tale, entitled 'The son of Kimanaueze and the daughter of Sun and Moon', as well as four illustrations of two Chokwe sculptures.

504 **A collection of Umbundu proverbs, adages and conundrums.**
Boston: West African Central Mission, 1914. 80p.
Contains over 500 short sayings of the Ovimbundu, in Umbundu, and mostly supplied with an English translation.

505 **The divining basket of the Ovimbundu.**
Leona Tucker. *Journal of the Royal Anthropological Institute*, vol. 70, no. 2 (1940), p. 171-201.
Describes the divining ritual used by traditional healers of the Ovimbundu, in which spirits are invoked using a divining basket (*ongombo*). Seventy-three items commonly found in such baskets are listed and described (some with photographs), as well as the types of spirit involved in the ritual.

506 **Epic tales of the Mbukushu.**
Thomas Larson. *African Studies*, vol. 22, no. 4 (1963), p. 176-89.
After a brief introduction to the Mbukushu, a people living in southern Angola along the Cubango river, as well as in Namibia and Botswana, nine of their folk tales are presented in English translation. Four of these deal with the Great Dikithi, a legendary hero who makes epic hunting expeditions. They were collected inside Botswana.

507 **Fables et contes angolais.** (Angolan stories and fables.)
Alfred Havenstein. Estella, Spain: Verbo Divino, 1976. 294p. bibliog.
(Studia Instituti Anthropos, no. 24).
A collection of 112 folk tales and customs, including myths and stories concerning ogres, giants, and extraordinary beings, as well tortoises, hares, and other animals. Many of the stories are of importance in traditional education, or concern witchcraft and spirits. They are translated into French from the original Chokwe, Umbundu, Kimbundu and Humbe.

508 **Folk tales of Angola.**
Edited by Héli Chatelain. New York: Negro University Press, 1969.
315p. maps.
This book contains fifty folk tales from Angola in the original Kimbundu, with English
translations, introduction and notes on the origin and significance of each story. First
published in 1894, in the *Journal of the American Folklore Society*, the stories are also
published in Portuguese (Lisbon: Agência-Geral do Ultramar, 1966, 570p.).

509 **Patterns of body movement in the music of boy's initiation in south-east**
**Angola.**
Gerhard Kubik. In: *The anthropology of the body*. Edited by John
Blacking. New York: Academic Press, 1988, p. 253-74.
This article explores the *Mukanda* ritual, one of the most important educational
institutions for many groups of central Africa. Dance is the primary concern, though
there is also information on music and instruments associated with the ritual.
Meticulous graphs and drawings are also included.

510 **Les symboles divinatoires: analyse socio-culturelle d'une technique de**
**divination des Cokwe d'Angola (Ngombo ya Cisuka).** (Divining symbols:
socio-cultural analysis of a technique for prophecy of the Chokwe of
Angola [Ngombo ya Cisuka].)
M. L. Rodrigues de Areia. Coimbra, Portugal: Instituto de
Antropologia, Universidade de Coimbra, 1985. 555p. bibliog.
A mammoth study of traditional religious symbols and practices used for prophecy and
soothsaying by the Chokwe group of Western Angola, which includes reference to the
work of early ethnographers, as well as the testimony of key informants. Religious
objects are described in detail, and a 'photographic dossier', containing 458
photographs, is included. There is also a lexicon of vernacular religious terms, and
many divining rituals are transcribed in their original language, as well as in French
translation.

**Dicionário Etimológico Bundo-Português.** (Etymological Umbundu-
Portuguese dictionary.)
*See* item no. 183.

**L'Angola traditionelle: une introduction aux problèmes magico-religieux.**
(Traditional Angola: an introduction to magical and religious problems.)
*See* item no. 211.

# Libraries, Museums and Archives

511  **The archives of Luanda, Angola.**
Joseph C. Miller. *International Journal of African History Studies*,
vol. 7, no. 4 (1974), p. 551-90.
A description of the main government and missionary archives of Luanda, based on
research visits to Angola from 1969-72. The article seeks to 'dispel illusions of a
documentary tropical treasure' in Angola.

512  **Arquivos de Angola.** (Angolan Archives.)
Luanda: Museu de Angola, 1933-49. tri-annual.
Periodical publication of the Museum of Angola, describing various historical
documents from the 16th to the 19th century. Includes statutes, decrees, biographies of
colonial figures, letters and other documentary ephemera on the economic, social and
political life of the colony.

513  **Canning House Library, Luso-Brazilian Council, London: author
catalogue A-Z and subject catalogue A-Z.**
Boston, Massachussets: G. K. Hall, 1967. 2 vols. First supplement,
1973, 288p.
Reproduces the card catalogue of the Canning House Library in London, which
contains a number of books and materials on Angola, as well as other parts of the
Portuguese and Spanish-speaking world.

514  **A catalog of the William B. Greenlee Collection of Portuguese history
and literature and the Portuguese materials in the Newberry Library.**
Compiled by Doris Varner Walsh.  Chicago: Newberry Library, 1953.
342p.
Includes a section covering material published up to 1950 on the Portuguese African
colonies.

515 **Directório dos centros de documentação e informação da República Popular de Angola.** (Directory of documentation and information centres in the People's Republic of Angola.) Centro de Informação Industrial, Ministério da Indústria. Luanda: Edição Corrigida, 1988. [27p.]

A full listing for nineteen documentation centres in Angola, providing addresses, hours of opening, facilities, services, publications and a summary of the documents available. A subject index, and an introductory note are also included.

516 **Documenting Portuguese Africa.** Ronald H. Chilcote. *Africana Newsletter*, vol. 1, no. 3 (summer 1963), p. 16-36.

This study covers serial publications, archives, libraries and institutions, with a bibliography of general works since 1945, and reference to some thirty-four political groups for Angola alone.

517 **Materials for west African history in Portuguese archives.** A. F. C. Ryder. London: Athlone Press, 1965. 92p.

Provides general information, as well as details of manuscript catalogues and indexes, for the most important Portuguese archives on west Africa, many of which include material on Angola. Archives covered include the important *Arquivo Nacional da Torre do Tombo*, the *Arquivo Historico Ultramarino*, and the archives and library of the Ministry of Foreign Affairs. Also listed are the *Biblioteca Nacional de Lisboa*, the *Biblioteca da Ajuda*, and the *Biblioteca Municipal do Porto*, and libraries at the *Academia das Ciências de Lisboa*, the *Sociedade de Geografia de Lisboa*, and the *Universidade de Coimbra*. This book formed part of a series: other works on archives in Belgium and Holland (Patricia Carson, 1962); Italy (Richard Gray and David Chambers, 1965); France (Patricia Carson, 1968); and the UK (Noel Matthews, 1973), all published by Athlone Press, are also of use to the student of Angolan history, insofar as several archives in these countries also contain relevant material on Angola.

518 **A note on the archives of the Propaganda Fide and the Capuchin archives for African history.** John K. Thornton. *History in Africa*, vol. 6 (1979), p. 341-44.

A description of the papal archive, *Archivio 'de Propaganda Fide'* in Rome, which holds numerous documents relating to the activities of Italian Capuchin clergy in the Kongo kingdom from the 17th century. Also includes information on other relevant archival sources in Italy on the Capuchins.

**Liberation movements in Lusophone Africa. Serials from the collection of Immanuel Wallerstein.**
*See* item no. 136.

**Libraries, Museums and Archives**

**Misiones capuchinas em Africa. Vol 1: La mision del Congo** (Capuchin missions in Africa. Vol 1: The Congo mission.)
*See* item no. 217.

**Monumenta missionaria Africana: Africa occidental.** (African missionary activity: West Africa.)
*See* item no. 218.

# Media

## Newspapers and magazines

519 **Africa.**
   Lisbon: Vozes do Tribo, 1986-91. weekly.
This weekly newspaper in Portuguese, which stopped publication in 1991, presented news and reports focused on Lusophone Africa.

520 **Africa 90.**
   Lisbon: Africa 90, 1990- . fortnightly.
A newly-established and reasonably comprehensive digest of news on Lusophone Africa, published in Portuguese, and covering politics, diplomacy, economy, culture, business and people. A separate section covers Angola. It is available on subscription from Africa 90, Rua dos Lusíadas, 5, 4°, 1300 Lisbon.

521 **Africa Hoje.** (Africa today.)
   Lisbon: Lucidus, 1986- . monthly.
A topical magazine dealing with Lusophone Africa, which includes news stories, in-depth articles and other features.

522 **Africa Mais.** (More Africa.)
   Lisbon: Epimark, 1991- . quarterly.
A new and glossy magazine that aims to go behind the news of Africa, investigating topics of political, economic and general interest. Prominence is given to Lusophone Africa, especially in a section of news updates, in which each of the Lusophone countries is featured separately.

**Media.** Newspapers and magazines

523  **Africa Notícias. Revista da Actualidade dos Países Africanos de Língua Oficial Portuguesa.** (Africa News. Review of Current Affairs in Lusophone Africa.)
Lisbon: João de Barros Publicações, 1985- . monthly.

A large and glossy monthly magazine covering news and in-depth reports on Lusophone Africa. The most recent special issue on Angola was in June 1988, although every issue includes a section on the country.

524  **Além-mar. Revista Missionária Mensual.** (Overseas. Monthly missionary magazine.)
Lisbon: Missionários Combonianos do Coração de Jesus, 1956- . monthly.

A monthly magazine of news and views aimed at Portuguese missionaries working overseas, and published by the Comboni Church of the Sacred Heart. Issue no. 349 (1988) is a special issue on Angola, whilst events in the country are reported on a regular basis.

525  **Angola na imprensa portuguesa. Abril e Maio de 1991.** (Angola in the Portuguese press. April and May, 1991.)
Lisbon: Centro de Informação e Difusão Amílcar Cabral (CIDAC), 1991. [n.p.].

A collection of newspaper articles, the majority from the Portuguese press, and dating back to the 1960s is held by CIDAC. This volume represents the selection from April and May, 1991, which was compiled as a report for an external agency.

526  **Angola. Revista.** (Angola. Review.)
Luanda: Liga Nacional Africana, 1932-75. fortnightly.

A left-wing review published during the colonial era, that included news, information on African resistence, as well as poetry and other items.

527  **Angola: Artes, Letras, Ideias e Economia.** (Angola: Arts, Humanities, Ideas, and Economy.)
Odivelas, Portugal: Angole, Artes Letras Ideias e Economia Lda, 1990- . monthly.

A new magazine in Portuguese, which presents news and criticism from the arts and humanities. The focus is on Angola, although articles are included on all of Lusophone Africa.

528  **Jornal de Angola.**
Luanda: Jornal de Angola.

The only daily newspaper in Angola at the time of compilation, as the official organ of the MPLA government. Circulation is estimated at around 41,000. However, recent relaxation of restrictions on the press suggests competition may reappear.

529 **Jornalismo de Angola: subsídios para a sua história.** (Journalism in Angola: elements towards its history.)
Luanda: Centro de Informação e Turismo de Angola, 1964. 127p.
A valuable survey of the press in 19th and 20th century Angola, albeit published from within the colonial establishment. Includes a list of journals published, and a section on African journalists.

530 **Notícia.** (News.)
Luanda; Lisbon: Neográfica, 1911-75. weekly.
A magazine published in Angola and Portugal during much of the colonial period, containing news and reports on Angola.

531 **Novembro. A Revista Angolana.** (November. The Angolan Review.)
Luanda: Edições Novembro, 1976-87. monthly.
A post-independence monthly topical magazine, which includes national news, and articles on issues of general interest. Included a section entitled *Documentação* (Documentation), which reproduced the text of speeches by prominent members of the government.

532 **Terra Solidária. Revista de Questões Internacionais.** (Land of Solidarity. Review of International Questions.)
Lisbon: Centro de Informação e Difusão Amílcar Cabral (CIDAC), 1986- . bi-monthly.
A general magazine devoted to news of liberation struggles, and events in countries recently liberated from colonialism. Has included articles on Angola, as well as the other Lusophone countries of Africa.

**Portuguese colonialism in Africa: the end of an era. The effects of Portuguese colonialism on education, science, culture and information.**
*See* item no. 444.

# Periodicals

533 **The African Communist. Journal of the South African Communist Party.**
Johannesburg: South African Communist Party, 1960- . quarterly.
Published until recently in London, this journal has included frequent reports and articles both on the anti-colonial struggle in Angola, and on the country's political development since independence.

## Media. Periodicals

534 **Africana.**
Oporto, Portugal: Centro de Estudos Africanos, Universidade
Portucalense, 1988- . irregular.

This journal, edited by the Centre for African Studies of the Universidade
Portucalense, covers a broad range of economics, history, social sciences and
development issues. It deals mainly, though not exclusively, with Lusophone Africa.
Papers are in Portuguese, with abstracts of articles in English and French.

535 **Boletim da Sociedade de Geografia de Lisboa.** (Bulletin of the
Geographical Society of Lisbon.)
Lisbon: Sociedade de Geografia de Lisboa, 1876- . bi-annual.

Mainly in Portuguese, this journal has contained numerous articles during its long
history on the both the geography of Angola, and of Portuguese settlement there.

536 **Estudos Portugueses e Africanos.** (Portuguese and African Studies.)
Campinas, Brazil: Universidade Estadual de Campinas, Instituto de
Estudos da Linguagem, 1984- . bi-annual.

Publishes reviews, essays, poems and short stories from or about Portugal or
Lusophone Africa. Since its inception, it has included frequent work on Angola,
including material from Angolan writers.

537 **Garcia de Orta.**
Lisbon: Instituto de Investigação Científica do Ultramar, 1953- .
annual

Published as one journal from 1953-72, separate series have run since then, covering
Anthropobiology (1982- ), Anthropology (1973- ), Botany (1973- ), Agronomy
(1973- ), Pharmacognosy (1973- ), Geography (1973- ), Geology (1973- ) and
Zoology (1973- ). Their appearance has been irregular since 1975. Although primarily
Portuguese-language journals, each series has included occasional articles on Angola in
both French and English.

538 **Journal of Southern African Studies.**
London: Oxford University Press, 1974- . quarterly.

An interdisciplinary journal of the social sciences focusing on southern Africa, which
regularly includes articles on Angola.

539 **Lavra e Oficina.** (Work and workplace.).
Luanda: União de Escritores Angolanos, 1978- . monthly.

A magazine in Portuguese devoted to arts and literature, with commentaries,
criticisms, news of events and original work by Angolan writers.

540 **Organization of Angolan Women. Bulletin.**
Luanda: Organização da Mulher Angolana, 1977-78. quarterly.

Short-lived information and news bulletin about Angolan women which included
poems and other writing on the situation of women. It was also published in French
and Portuguese.

146

541 **Portugal em Africa. Revista de Cultura Missionária.** (Portugal in Africa. Journal of Missionary Culture.)
Lisbon: Editorial LIAM, 1894-1971. bi-monthly.
A journal aimed at missionaries in Portuguese Africa, with articles relating directly to missionary activity, as well as others that dealt more generally with the society and culture of the African territories.

542 **Portuguese Studies.**
Edited by the Department of Portuguese and Brazilian Studies, Kings College London. London: Modern Humanities Research Association, 1985- . annual.
A journal concerned with the literature and culture of the Portuguese-speaking world, with occasional articles on Angola. Each issue also includes a bibliography of recent books and articles, subdivided by discipline and by country.

543 **Portuguese Studies Newsletter.**
Edited by Douglas L. Wheeler. Durham, New Hampshire: International Conference Group on Modern Portugal, 1976- . irregular.
Includes information on the group's activities, and bibliographic material that covers Angola.

544 **Presence Africaine: Revue Culturelle du Monde Noir/Cultural Review of the Negro World.**
Paris: Société Africaine de Culture, 1947- . (bilingual edition, 1967- .) quarterly.
The aim of this journal is to sensitize African peoples in their fight for cultural identity and development. It provides a range of material written by artists and social scientists in English and French, and during the 1960s and 1970s, included many articles on the struggle for independence in Angola and other Portuguese territories. More recently, articles on Angola have been rare. An analytical index for the period 1947-72 was produced by Femi Ojo-Ade (New York: Three Continents Press, 1977), although there is no separate index by country.

545 **Revista Internacional de Estudos Africanos.** (International Journal of African Studies.)
Lisbon: Instituto de Investigação Científica Tropical, Centro de Estudos Africanos e Asiáticos. 1984- . bi-annual.
The major Portuguese-language journal of African studies, covering mainly history and the social sciences, but also to a lesser extent the wider field of the humanities, including literary criticism.

# Directories and Current Reference Sources

546   **Africa Confidential.**
London: Miramoor, 1960- . fortnightly.
A useful source of information on political and economic events, containing both news reports, and short articles, generally aimed at a business audience.

547   **Africa Contemporary Record.**
Edited by Colin Legum.   London: Rex Collings, 1969- . annual.
Each volume of this journal is divided into three parts. The first presents essays on current issues, followed in part 2 by a country-by-country review of the year's events. This includes information on political, social, economic and foreign affairs. Finally, in part 3, documents not readily available elsewhere are presented, including speeches, treaties, accords, etc. This is an important reference text, and its coverage of Angola is excellent.

548   **Africa Research Bulletin.**
Exeter, England: Africa Research Ltd, 1964- . monthly.
Separate political and economic series provide a digest of news and current affairs from Africa, and serve as a useful source of information on developments in Angola.

549   **Africa Review.**
Saffron Walden, England: Walden Publishing, 1977- .
Provides a review of the year's events in each African country, including key economic indicators, a profile of the economy, and a guide to business information.

550 **Provisional list of non-governmental organizations active in the field of disaster relief and rehabilitation in Angola.**
United Nations Disaster Relief Organization (UNDRO). Geneva: Office of the UN Disaster Relief Coordinator, 1988. 18p.
Lists 18 foreign NGOs (Non-Governmental Organizations) which were operational in Angola in 1988.

# Bibliographies

551 **Africana: bibliographie sur l'Afrique luso-hispanique [1800-1980].**
(Africana: bibliography about Luso-Hispanic Africa [1880-1980].)
René Pélissier.   Orgeval, France: Editions Pélissier, 1980. 205p.
A critical annotated bibliography in French, containing 121 references to Angola. The works cited are in a variety of European languages.

552 **Angola: a selected bibliography 1960-1965.**
Manfred W. Werner.   Washington, DC: United States Library of Congress, 1965.
A general bibliography, which includes many articles in English.

553 **Bibliografia das literaturas africanas de expressão portuguesa.**
(Bibliography of African literature in Portuguese.)
Gerald Moser, Manuel Ferreira.   Lisbon: Imprensa Nacional/Casa da Moeda, 1983. 2nd ed. 405p.
This essential bibliography is divided into four sections, covering oral traditions; 'art literature' (i.e. novels, novellas, tales, prose sketches, theatre and poetry); literary history and criticism; and finally literary periodicals. In each section, there is separate coverage of each country, as well as a section on works on Lusophone Africa as a whole. The entries are in Portuguese, but each section contains an introduction in English. There is also an extensive biographical index, a chronology of cultural events for each country (in English), and an author/title index. The bibliography covers works up to 1979.

Bibliographies

554 **Bibliografia das publicações recentes sobre a Africa de Língua Oficial Portuguesa.** (Bibliography of recent publications about Lusophone Africa.) Jill R. Dias. *Revista Internacional de Estudos Africanos*, vol. 12/13 (1990), p. 501-24.
Includes over seventy recent references on Angola, divided into sections on politics, economy, culture, etc. There are also other relevant sections on Lusophone Africa as a whole, and Portuguese foreign policy towards the region.

555 **Bibliografia geológica do ultramar português.** (Geological bibliography of the Portuguese overseas territories.) Francisco Gonçalves, Jaime Carneiro. Lisbon: Junta de Investigações do Ultramar, 1959. 272p.
Entries include a brief abstract, and are arranged by author, with an area, author and subject index.

556 **Bibliografia sobre a economia portuguesa.** (Bibliography on the Portuguese economy.) Lisbon: Instituto Nacional da Estatística, Centro de Estudos Económicos, 1948- . annual.
Until 1974, this bibliography covered all of the Portuguese overseas territories, representing a useful source for material on the colonial Angolan economy. The bibliography is arranged by country, and subdivided by subject. It includes periodicals, newspapers and monographs.

557 **Bibliographie de l'Angola (Biblioteca Angolensis) 1500-1910.** (Bibliography of Angola 1500-1910.) Paul Borchardt. Brussels: Institut de Sociologie, 1912. 61p.
Cites over one thousand references mainly on economics and geography.

558 **Catálogo de publicações.** (Catalogue of publications.) Instituto de Investigação Científica Tropical (IICT). Lisbon: IICT, 1987. 304p.
A list of articles published in the various journals of the IICT, and its predecessor, the Junta de Investigações Científicas do Ultramar, between 1946 and 1986. The publications include *Anais* (1946-60), *Boletim do Filmoteca Ultramarina Portuguesa* (1954-71), *Colóquios* (1949-50), *Estudos de Antropologia Cultural* (1965-81); *Estudos das Ciências Políticas e Sociais* (1956-72); *Estudos, Ensaios e Documentos* (1954-86); *Estudos de História e Cartografia Antiga* (1963-85); *Garcia de Orta* (1953-86: see item no. 537); *Index Seminum* (1949-83); *Leba* (1978-82: see item no. 57); *Memórias* (1943-85); *Religiões e Missões* (1967-69); *Separatas* (1961-85); and *Studia* (1958-81), as well as occasional publications.

151

# Bibliographies

559 **Contribuição para uma bibliografia sobre o quaternário e pré-história de Angola.** (Contribution to a bibliography on the Quaternary and prehistory of Angola.)
Lívia Ferrão. *Leba* (Lisbon), vol. 6 (1987), p. 81-86.

Includes 102 references on the Quaternary and pre-history of Angola, most of which are in Portuguese, but with a significant number in either English or French. It was submitted for publication in 1983.

560 **Emerging nationalism in Portuguese Africa: a bibliography of documentary references through 1965.**
Ronald H. Chilcote. Stanford, California: Hoover Institution on War, Revolution and Peace, 1969. 114p. (Hoover Institution Bibliographical Series, no. 39).

Deals with material issued by Portuguese African nationalist movements from 1959-65, and stored on microfilm in the Hoover Institution Library. Transcriptions of a number of these documents are contained in *Emerging nationalism in Portuguese Africa: documents* (q.v). Includes over 45 pages of references to Angola.

561 **Informação Bibliográfica.** (Bibliographic Information.)
Lisbon: Centro de Informação e Documentação Amílcar Cabral (CIDAC), 1989- . bi-monthly.

Provides information on recent acquisitions at CIDAC, an important documentation centre for Lusophone Africa as a whole. The titles are listed alphabetically, with an author and country index. There is also a list of the 95 serial titles available at the centre.

562 **International African Bibliography: current books, articles and papers in African studies.**
Compiled and edited by David Hall, in association with the Centre of African Studies at the Library, School of Oriental and African Studies, University of London. London: Mansell, 1971- . quarterly.

A general bibliographic update on Africa, divided by region and country, and for Africa as a whole, by subject area. Each entry includes a list of keywords and every edition includes a subject index. Five year compilations began in 1978.

563 **A nutrição no ultramar português. Subsídio para uma bibliografia.**
(Nutrition in the Portuguese overseas territories. A contribution towards a bibliography.)
Carlos Santos Reis. Lisbon: Instituto Nacional de Estatística, Centro de Estudos Demográficos, 1973. 243p.

An annotated bibliography of work on nutrition in the Portuguese colonies, with 162 references to Angola.

564  **Portuguese Africa: a guide to official publications.**
Mary Jane Gibson.  Washington, DC: Library of Congress, 1967.
217p.

This reference work contains 2,831 entries of official publications, mostly in
Portuguese, with each entry providing full bibliographic information, as well as the
source from which the work can be obtained. The section on Angola comprises 611
entries, most published by the Imprensa Nacional in Luanda.

565  **Portuguese-speaking Africa 1900-1979: a select bibliography. Volume 1:
Angola.**
Susan Jean Gowan.  Braamfontein, South Africa: South African
Institute of International Affairs, 1982. 346p. maps. (Bibliographical
series, no. 9).

Includes over 2,300 references on Angola this century. For both the pre- and post-
independence periods, there is a general section (including bibliographies), and
sections on politics and government (including liberation movements and the civil
war), foreign relations, and aspects of economics and development (including
agriculture).

**Angola: bibliografia antropológica.** (Angola: anthropological bibliography.)
*See* item no. 150.

**Portuguese Studies.**
*See* item no. 542.

**Portuguese Studies Newsletter.**
*See* item no. 543.

# Indexes

There follow three separate indexes: authors (personal and corporate); titles; and subjects. Title entries are italicized and refer either to the main titles, or to other works cited in the annotations. The numbers refer to bibliographic entries, not to pages. Individual index entries are arranged in alphabetical sequence.

# Index of Authors

157

159

# Index of Titles

# M

# N

# O

# P

# Index of Subjects

# Map of Angola

This map shows the more important towns and other features.

CONGO

R. Zaire

R. Kwango

CABINDA
Cabinda

M'Banza Congo

ZAIRE

UIGE
Uige

ZAIRE

Lucapa

BENGO

LUNDA
NORTE

Luanda

2
N'dalatando

MALANJE

Saurimo

4

Malanje

R. Cuanza

LUNDA
SUL

CUANZA
SUL

R. Lui.

Sumbe

BIE

Luena

Benguela

3
Huambo

Kuito

MOXICO

1

Menongue

R. Cuando

Namibe

HUILA

ZAMBIA

NAMIBE

Lubango

Cassinga

CUANDO
CUBANGO

CUNENE
Ondjiva

NAMIBIA

Miles
0          200

—·—·—  National Boundary
--------  District Boundary
------  Railway

1  BENGUELA
2  CUANZA NORTE
3  HUAMBO
4  LUANDA